Summary

Congress has received President Obama's budget request for FY2013 which includes ~~$140.820~~ billion for research and development (R&D), a $1.951 billion (1.4%) increase from the FY2012 estimated funding level of $138.869 billion. The request represents the President's R&D priorities; Congress may opt to agree with part or all of the request, or may express different priorities through the appropriations process. In particular, Congress will play a central role in determining the extent to which the federal R&D investment can grow in the context of increased pressure on discretionary spending and how available funding will be prioritized and allocated. Low or negative growth in the overall R&D investment may require movement of resources across disciplines, programs, or agencies to address priorities.

Funding for R&D is highly concentrated in a few departments. Under President Obama's FY2013 budget request, seven federal agencies would receive 95.8% of total federal R&D funding, with the Department of Defense (50.6%) and the Department of Health and Human Services (22.3%, primarily for the National Institutes of Health) accounting for nearly three-fourths of all R&D funding.

Among the largest changes proposed in the President's request, the R&D budget of the Department of Defense would fall by $1.535 billion (-2.1%), while R&D funding for the Department of Commerce's National Institute of Standards and Technology (NIST) would increase by $1.329 billion. The NIST growth is fueled by increases in funding for its core research laboratories and by the establishment of two new initiatives: $1 billion for the National Network for Manufacturing Innovation, which seeks to promote the development of manufacturing technologies with broad applications, and $300 million for a Wireless Innovation (WIN) Fund to help develop cutting-edge technologies for public safety users.

President Obama has requested increases in the R&D budgets of NIST, the National Science Foundation, and the Department of Energy's Office of Science that were targeted for doubling over 7 years, from their FY2006 levels, by the America COMPETES Act, and over 10 years by the America COMPETES Reauthorization Act of 2010. The funding requested for FY2013 is consistent with a doubling timeframe of 17 years, much longer than authorized by either act.

The President's budget request continues support for three multi-agency R&D initiatives in FY2013, proposing $1.766 billion for the National Nanotechnology Initiative, an increase of $70 million (4.1%) over FY2012; $3.807 billion for the Networking and Information Technology Research and Development program, an increase of $69 million (1.8%); and $2.633 billion for the U.S. Global Change Research Program, an increase of $136 million (5.6%).

In recent years, Congress has used a variety of mechanisms to complete the annual appropriations process after the start of the fiscal year. This may affect agencies' execution of their R&D budgets, including delaying or canceling some planned R&D and equipment acquisition.

Contents

Figures

Tables

Contacts

Overview

The 112th Congress continues to take a strong interest in the health of the U.S. research and development (R&D) enterprise and in providing support for federal R&D activities. However, widespread concerns about the federal debt and recent and projected federal budget deficits are driving difficult decisions involving prioritization of R&D within the context of the entire federal budget and among competing priorities within the federal R&D portfolio. The U.S. government supports a broad range of scientific and engineering research and development. Its purposes include addressing specific concerns such as national defense, health, safety, the environment, and energy security; advancing knowledge generally; developing the scientific and engineering workforce; and strengthening U.S. innovation and competitiveness in the global economy. Most of the R&D funded by the federal government is performed in support of the unique missions of the funding agencies. The federal government has played an important role in supporting R&D efforts that have led to scientific breakthroughs and new technologies, from jet aircraft and the Internet to communications satellites and defenses against disease.

Congress will play a central role in defining the nation's R&D priorities as it makes decisions with respect to the size and distribution of aggregate, agency, and programmatic R&D funding. Some Members of Congress have expressed concerns about the level of federal funding in light of the current federal fiscal condition, deficit, and debt. As Congress acts to complete the FY2013 appropriations process it faces two overarching issues: the extent to which the federal R&D investment can grow in the context of increased pressure on discretionary spending and how available funding will be prioritized and allocated. Low or negative growth in the overall R&D investment may require movement of resources across disciplines, programs, or agencies to address priorities.

President Obama's proposed FY2013 budget, released on February 13, 2012, includes $140.820 billion for R&D in FY2013, a 1.4% increase over the estimated FY2012 R&D funding level of $138.869 billion.[1] Adjusted for inflation, the President's FY2013 R&D request represents a decrease of 0.2% from the FY2012 level.[2] This report provides government-wide, multi-agency, and individual agency analyses of the President's FY2013 request as it relates to R&D and related activities.

Among its provisions, the President's proposed FY2013 R&D funding maintains an emphasis on increasing funding for the physical sciences and engineering, an effort consistent with the intent of the America COMPETES Act (P.L. 110-69) and the America COMPETES Reauthorization Act of 2010 (P.L. 111-358). These acts seek to achieve this objective by authorizing increased funding for accounts at three agencies with a strong R&D emphasis in these disciplines: the Department of Energy Office of Science, the National Science Foundation, and the Department of Commerce National Institute of Standards and Technology's core laboratory research and R&D facilities construction funding (collectively referred to as the "targeted accounts"). Appropriations provided to these agencies have fallen short of the levels authorized in P.L. 110-69. (See "

---

[1] Funding levels included in this document are in current dollars unless otherwise noted. Inflation diminishes the purchasing power of federal R&D funds, so an increase that does not equal or exceed the inflation rate may reduce real purchasing power.

[2] As calculated by CRS using the GDP (chained) price index from Table 10.1, Gross Domestic Product and Deflators Used in the Historical Tables: 1940–2017, from the President's FY2013 budget. Available at http://www.whitehouse.gov/sites/default/files/omb/budget/fy2013/assets/hist10z1 xls.

Multiagency R&D Initiatives" for detailed information.)

More broadly, in a 2009 speech before members of the National Academy of Sciences, President Obama put forth a goal of increasing the national investment in R&D to more than 3% of the U.S. gross domestic product (GDP). President Obama did not provide details on how this goal might be achieved (e.g., how much would be funded through increases in direct federal R&D funding or through indirect mechanisms such as the research and experimentation (R&E) tax credit[3]); however, doing so likely would require a substantial increase in public and/or private investment. In 2009, total U.S. R&D expenditures were $400.458 billion,[4] or approximately 2.87% of GDP.[5] Based on 2009 figures, reaching President Obama's 3% goal would have required an increase of 4.4% in national R&D spending.

In addition, advocates for increased federal R&D funding—including President Obama's science advisor, John Holdren—have raised concerns about the potential harm of a "boom-bust" approach to federal R&D funding (i.e., rapid growth in federal R&D funding followed by much slower growth, flat funding, or even decline).[6] The biomedical research community experienced a variety of challenges resulting from such a circumstance following the five-year doubling of the National Institutes of Health (NIH) budget that was completed in FY2003. With the NIH doubling came a rapid expansion of the nation's biomedical research infrastructure (e.g., buildings, laboratories, equipment), as well as rapid growth in university faculty hiring, students pursuing biomedical degrees, and grant applications to NIH. After the doubling, however, the agency's budget fell each year in real terms from FY2004 to FY2009. Critics assert there have been a variety of damages from this boom-bust cycle, including interruptions and cancellations of promising research, declining share in the number of NIH grant proposals funded, decreased student interest in pursuing graduate studies, and reduced employment prospects for the large number of biomedical researchers with advanced degrees. According to then-NIH Director Elias Zerhouni, the damages have been particularly acute for early- and mid-career scientists seeking a first or second grant.[7] The current effort to double funding for the targeted accounts has followed a similar pattern, but on a smaller scale. Funding for the targeted accounts grew by about 28% from FY2006 to FY2010 (or approximately 6.4% per year), but has been essentially flat since then.

Analysis of federal R&D funding is complicated by several factors, such as inconsistency among agencies in the reporting of R&D and the inclusion of R&D in accounts with non-R&D activities. As a result of these and other factors, the R&D agency figures reported by the White House Office of Management and Budget (OMB) and White House Office of Science and Technology

---

[3] The research and experimentation tax credit is frequently referred to as the research and development tax credit or R&D tax credit, through the credit does not apply to development expenditures. For additional information about the R&E tax credit, see CRS Report RL31181, *Research Tax Credit: Current Law, Legislation in the 112th Congress, and Policy Issues*, by Gary Guenther.

[4] Preliminary estimate of 2009 U.S. R&D expenditures, National Science Foundation, *National Patterns of R&D Resources:2008*, NSF 10-314, Arlington, VA, March 2010, http://www.nsf.gov/statistics/nsf10314/.

[5] Based on 2009 U.S. GDP of $14,369.1 billion as reported by the U.S. Department of Commerce Bureau of Economic Analysis, *National Income and Product Accounts Table*, Table 1.1.5, http://www.bea.gov/national/nipaweb/TableView.asp?SelectedTable=5&Freq=Qtr&FirstYear=2007&LastYear=2009.

[6] Jennifer Couzin and Greg Miller, "NIH Budget: Boom and Bust," *Science*, vol. 316, no. 5823 (April 2007), pp. 356-361, at http://www.scienceonline.org/cgi/content/full/316/5823/356.

[7] Ibid. For additional information on NIH R&D funding issues, see CRS Report R41705, *The National Institutes of Health (NIH): Organization, Funding, and Congressional Issues*, by Judith A. Johnson and Pamela W. Smith.

Policy (OSTP), and shown in **Table 1**, may differ somewhat from the agency budget analyses that appear later in this report.

Another factor complicating analysis of the President's FY2013 budget request is the inclusion of the Wireless Innovation (WIN) Fund, a part of the Administration's Wireless Innovation and Infrastructure Initiative. First proposed in the President's FY2012 budget request, the WIN Fund would receive $300 million in FY2013 from receipts generated through electromagnetic spectrum auctions. The fund would support development of leading-edge wireless technologies and applications for public safety. Under the President's budget, if the WIN Fund is established, the National Institute of Standards and Technology (NIST) would receive up to $300 million in FY2013. NIST intends to use these funds to work with industry and public safety organizations on research and development of new standards, technologies, and applications that advance public safety communications, including establishing a competitive grant fund. The grant fund would award between $70 and $75 million per year from FY2014 through FY2016 for related research, development, and demonstration projects.[8]

Federal R&D Funding Perspectives

Federal R&D funding can be analyzed from a variety of perspectives that provide different insights.

Agency Perspective

The authorization and appropriations process views federal R&D funding primarily from agency and program perspectives. **Table 1** provides data on R&D by agency for FY2011 (actual), FY2012 (estimated), and FY2013 (request) as reported by OMB.

Under President Obama's FY2013 budget request, seven federal agencies would receive 95.8% of total federal R&D funding: Department of Defense (DOD), 50.6%; Department of Health and Human Services (HHS) (primarily the National Institutes of Health), 22.3%; Department of Energy (DOE), 8.5%; National Aeronautics and Space Administration (NASA), 6.8%; National Science Foundation (NSF), 4.2%; Department of Commerce (DOC), 1.8%; and Department of Agriculture (USDA), 1.6%. This report provides an analysis of the R&D budget requests for these agencies, as well as for the Department of Homeland Security (DHS), Department of the Interior (DOI), Department of Transportation (DOT), and the Environmental Protection Agency (EPA). In total, these agencies account for more than 98% of current and requested federal R&D funding.

The largest agency R&D increases in the President's FY2013 request are for DOC, $1.315 billion (104.5%);[9] DOE, $884 million (8.0%); HHS, $247 million (0.8%); NSF, $224 million (3.9%);

---

[8] *Wireless Innovation Fund,* factsheet, National Institute of Standards and Technology website, http://www.nist.gov/public_affairs/factsheet/wireless_innov2013.cfm.

[9] The Department of Commerce total includes mandatory proposals for the Wireless Innovation Network and the National Network for Manufacturing Innovation at the National Institute for Standards and Technology. These programs are discussed in the DOC NIST section of this report. Mandatory spending is typically provided in permanent or multi-year appropriations contained in the authorizing law, and therefore, the funding becomes available automatically each year, without legislative action by Congress. For additional information on mandatory spending, see (continued...)

---

and NASA, $203 million (2.2%). Under President Obama's FY2013 budget request, DOD R&D funding would be reduced by $1.535 billion (-2.1%) and USDA R&D by $34 million (-1.5%).

Table 1. Federal Research and Development Funding by Agency, FY2011-FY2013

(Budget authority, dollar amounts in millions)

Department/Agency	FY2011 Actual	FY2012 Estimate	FY2013 Request	Dollar Change, 2012 to 2013	Percent Change, 2012 to 2013
Defense	77,500	72,739	71,204	-1,535	-2.1%
Health and Human Services	31,186	31,153	31,400	247	0.8%
Energy	10,673	11,019	11,903	884	8.0%
NASA	9,099	9,399	9,602	203	2.2%
National Science Foundation	5,486	5,680	5,904	224	3.9%
Commerce	1,275	1,258	2,573	1,315	104.5%
Agriculture	2,135	2,331	2,297	-34	-1.5%
Veterans Affairs	1,160	1164	1166	2	0.2%
Transportation	953	944	1,076	132	14.0%
Interior	757	796	854	58	7.3%
Homeland Security	664	577	729	152	26.3%
Environmental Protection Agency	584	568	580	12	2.1%
Other	1,242	1,241	1,532	291	23.4%
Total[a]	**142,714**	**138,869**	**140,820**	**1,951**	**1.4%**

Source: Executive Office of the President, OMB, *Analytical Perspectives, Budget of the United States Government, Fiscal Year 2013,* Table 22-1.

a.   Totals may differ from the sum of the components due to rounding.

Character of Work, Facilities, and Equipment Perspective

Federal R&D funding can also be examined by the character of work it supports—basic research, applied research, and development—and funding provided for facilities and acquisition of major R&D equipment. (See **Table 2**.) President Obama's FY2013 request includes $30.627 billion for basic research, up $449 million (1.5%) from FY2012; $33.369 billion for applied research, up $1.586 billion (5.0%); $74.138 billion for development, down $345 million (-0.5%); and $2.690 billion for facilities and equipment, up $265 million (10.9%).

(...continued)

CRS Report RL33074, *Mandatory Spending Since 1962*, by D. Andrew Austin and Mindy R. Levit.

Table 2. Federal Research and Development Funding by Character of Work, Facilities, and Equipment, FY2011-FY2013

(Budget authority, dollar amounts in millions)

	FY2011 Actual	FY2012 Estimate	FY2013 Request	Dollar Change, 2012 to 2013	Percent Change, 2012 to 2013
Basic research	29,697	30,178	30,627	449	1.5%
Applied research	30,833	31,783	33,369	1,586	5.0%
Development	80,246	74,483	74,138	-345	-0.5%
Facilities and equipment	1,938	2,425	2,690	265	10.9%
Total[a]	142,714	138,869	140,820	1,951	1.4%

Source: Executive Office of the President, OMB, *Analytical Perspectives, Budget of the United States Government, Fiscal Year 2013*, Table 22-1.

a.   Totals may differ from the sum of the components due to rounding.

Combined Perspective

Combining these perspectives, federal R&D funding can be viewed in terms of each agency's contribution to basic research, applied research, development, and facilities and equipment. (See **Table 3**.) In turn, the overall federal R&D budget reflects a wide range of national priorities, from supporting advances in spaceflight to developing new and affordable sources of energy. These priorities and the mission of each agency contribute, in part, to the composition of an agency's R&D spending (i.e., the allocation between basic research, applied research, development, and facilities and equipment). The federal government is the nation's largest supporter of basic research, funding 53.2% of U.S. basic research in 2009, primarily because the private sector asserts it cannot capture an adequate return on long-term fundamental research investments. In contrast, industry funded only 21.7% of U.S. basic research in 2009 (with state governments, universities, and other non-profit organizations funding the remaining 25.1%).[10] In the President's FY2013 budget request, the Department of Health and Human Services, primarily the National Institutes of Health (NIH), accounts for more than half of all federal funding for basic research.[11]

In contrast to basic research, industry is the primary funder of applied research in the United States, accounting for an estimated 48.1% in 2009, while the federal government accounted for an estimated 42.2%.[12] Among federal agencies, HHS is the largest funder of applied research, accounting for nearly half of all federally funded applied research in the President's FY2013 budget request.[13] Industry also provides the vast majority of funding for development. Industry

---

[10] National Science Board, *Science and Engineering Indicators 2012*, NSB 12-01, Appendix Table 4-8, January 2012, http://www.nsf.gov/statistics/seind12/appendix.htm.

[11] Executive Office of the President, Office of Management and Budget, *Analytical Perspectives, Budget of the United States Government, Fiscal Year 2012*, Table 22-1, February 14, 2011.

[12] National Science Board, *Science and Engineering Indicators 2012*, NSB 12-01, Appendix Table 4-9, January 2012, http://www.nsf.gov/statistics/seind12/appendix.htm.

[13] Executive Office of the President, Office of Management and Budget, *Analytical Perspectives*, Table 22-1, February 13, 2012, http://www.whitehouse.gov/sites/default/files/omb/budget/fy2013/assets/spec.pdf.

accounted for an estimated 77.6% in 2009, while the federal government provided an estimated 21.3%.[14] DOD is the primary federal agency funder of development, accounting for 87.0% of total federal development funding in the President's FY2013 budget request.[15]

Table 3. Top R&D Funding Agencies by Character of Work, Facilities and Equipment, FY2011-FY2013

(Budget authority, dollar amounts in millions)

	FY2011 Actual	FY2012 Estimated	FY2013 Request	Dollar Change, 2012 to 2013	Percent Change, 2012 to 2013
Basic Research					
Health and Human Services	16,013	16,051	16,010	-41	-0.3%
National Science Foundation	4,636	4,778	4,987	209	4.4%
Energy	3,979	3,918	4,096	178	4.5%
Applied Research					
Health and Human Services	15,066	14,919	15,192	273	1.8%
Defense	4,328	4,737	4,477	-260	-5.5%
Energy	3,575	3,857	4,152	295	7.6%
Development					
Defense	71,205	65,786	64,536	-1,250	-1.9%
NASA	5,299	4,975	5,131	156	3.1%
Energy	2,361	2,387	2,855	468	19.6%
Facilities and Equipment					
Energy	758	857	800	-57	-6.7%
Commerce	254	209	632	423	202.4%
National Science Foundation	395	452	458	6	1.3%

Source: Executive Office of the President, OMB, *Analytical Perspectives, Budget of the United States Government, Fiscal Year 2013, February 13, 2012.*

Note: Top funding agencies based on FY2013 request.

---

[14] National Science Board, *Science and Engineering Indicators 2012*, NSB 12-01, Appendix Table 4-10, January 2012, http://www.nsf.gov/statistics/seind12/appendix.htm.

[15] Executive Office of the President, Office of Management and Budget, *Analytical Perspectives,* Table 22-1, February 13, 2012.

Multiagency R&D Initiatives

Federal R&D funding can also be viewed in terms of multiagency efforts, such as the National Nanotechnology Initiative and presidential initiatives. President Obama's FY2013 budget request provides funding for six multiagency R&D initiatives discussed below.

Doubling Effort

In 2006, President Bush announced his American Competitiveness Initiative which, in part, sought to increase federal funding for physical sciences and engineering research by doubling funding over 10 years (FY2006-FY2016) for targeted accounts at three agencies—NSF, all; DOE, Office of Science only; and NIST, the scientific and technical research and services (STRS) and construction of research facilities (CRF) accounts.

In 2007, Congress authorized substantial increases for these targeted accounts under the America COMPETES Act (P.L. 110-69), setting aggregate authorization levels for FY2008-FY2010 consistent with a more aggressive seven-year doubling pace.[16] However, funding provided for these agencies in the Consolidated Appropriations Act, 2008 (P.L. 110-161), the Omnibus Appropriations Act, 2009 (P.L. 111-8), and the Consolidated Appropriations Act, 2010 (P.L. 111-117) fell below these targets.[17] (See **Table 4** for individual and aggregate appropriations for the targeted accounts.)

In 2010, Congress passed the America COMPETES Reauthorization Act of 2010 (P.L. 111-358) which, among other things, authorized appropriations levels for the targeted accounts for FY2011-FY2013.[18] The aggregate authorization levels in this act for the targeted accounts are consistent with an 11-year doubling path, slower than the America COMPETES Act's 7-year doubling path. Moreover, aggregate FY2012 funding for the targeted accounts was approximately $12.529 billion, $1.631 billion less than authorized in the act, setting a pace to double over 17 years from the FY2006 level—more than twice the length of time originally envisioned in the 2007 America COMPETES Act and more than half longer than the doubling period established by the America COMPETES Reauthorization Act of 2010.[19]

In his FY2013 budget, President Obama is requesting $13.073 billion in aggregate funding for the targeted accounts, an increase of $544.0 million (4.3%) above the enacted FY2012 aggregate funding level of $12.529 billion, but below the America COMPETES Reauthorization Act of 2010 (P.L. 111-358) level of $15.105 billion. The President's request for each of the targeted accounts is less than authorized by P.L. 111-358:

---

[16] For additional information, see CRS Report RL34328, *America COMPETES Act: Programs, Funding, and Selected Issues*, by Deborah D. Stine.

[17] In 2009, the American Recovery and Reinvestment Act of 2009 (P.L. 111-5) provided supplemental funding for several targeted accounts (approximately $5.202 billion).

[18] For additional information, see CRS Report R41231, *America COMPETES Reauthorization Act of 2010 (H.R. 5116) and the America COMPETES Act (P.L. 110-69): Selected Policy Issues*, coordinated by Heather B. Gonzalez.

[19] All doubling path calculations in this report use FY2006 as the baseline. For additional information on the doubling effort, see CRS Report R41951, *An Analysis of Efforts to Double Federal Funding for Physical Sciences and Engineering Research*, by John F. Sargent Jr.

- The President is requesting $7.373 billion for NSF for FY2013; P.L. 111-358 authorizes $8.300 billion.

- The FY2013 request for DOE's Office of Science is $4.992 billion; P.L. 111-358 authorizes $6.007 billion.

- With respect to the targeted accounts at the NIST:

  - President Obama is requesting $648.0 million for NIST core laboratory research[20] for FY2013; P.L. 111-358 authorizes $676.7 million.

  - The President is requesting $60.0 million for NIST construction of research facilities for FY2013;[21] P.L. 111-358 authorizes $121.3 million.

In light of budget constraints, the future of the doubling path appears to be in question. In his FY2010 *Plan for Science and Innovation,* President Obama stated that he, like President Bush, would seek to double funding for basic research over 10 years (FY2006 to FY2016) at the ACI agencies.[22] In his FY2011 budget documents, President Obama extended the period over which he intended to double these agencies' budgets to 11 years (FY2006 to FY2017).[23] The FY2013 budget request, like the FY2012 budget request, reiterates President Obama's intention to double funding for the targeted accounts from their FY2006 levels but does not specify the length of time over which the doubling is to take place. In addition, the Office of Management and Budget's Public Budget Database, published as part of the President's FY2013 request, includes projections of budget authority for the targeted accounts through FY2017; projected FY2017 funding for the targeted accounts sets a doubling pace of more than 21 years.

Table 4. Funding for Targeted Accounts
FY2006-FY2011 (Actual), FY2012 (Estimated), and FY2013 (Request)

(in millions of current dollars)

Agency	FY2006 Actual	FY2007 Actual	FY2008 Actual	FY2009 Actual	FY2009 ARRA	FY2010 Actual	FY2011 Actual	FY2012 Est.	FY2013 Request
NSF	5,646	5,884	6,084	6,469	2,402	6,972	6,913a	7,033	7,373
DOE/Office of Science	3,632	3,837	4,083	4,807	1,633	4,964	4,843	4,874	4,992
NIST/core researchb	395	434	441	472	220	515	497.4	567	648
NIST/facilities	174	59	161	172	360	147	70	55	60
Totalc	9,846	10,214	10,768	11,920	4,615	12,598	12,323	12,529	13,073

Source: NIST, budget requests for FY2008-FY2013, available at http://www.nist.gov/public_affairs/budget/index.cfm; DOE, budget requests for FY2008-FY2013, available at http://www.cfo.doe.gov/crorgcf30.htm; NSF, budget requests for FY2008-FY2013 available at http://www.nsf.gov/about/budget.

---

[20] NIST core laboratory research is the Scientific and Technical Research and Services (STRS) account.

[21] Executive Office of the President, Office of Science and Technology Policy, *Innovation, Education, and Infrastructure*, February 14, 2011, http://www.whitehouse.gov/sites/default/files/microsites/ostp/FY12-rd-fs.pdf.

[22] Executive Office of the President, Office of Science and Technology Policy, *The President's Plan for Science and Innovation: Doubling Funding for Key Basic Research Agencies in the 2010 Budget*, May 7, 2009, http://www.whitehouse.gov/files/documents/ostp/budget/doubling.pdf.

[23] Executive Office of the President, Office of Science and Technology Policy, *The President's Plan for Science and Innovation: Doubling Funding for Key Basic Research Agencies in the 2011 Budget*, February 1, 2010, http://www.whitehouse.gov/sites/default/files/doubling%2011%20final.pdf.

a. Includes $54.0 million transferred to the U.S. Coast Guard for icebreaking services (per P.L. 112-10).

b. NIST core research is performed under its scientific and technical research and services (STRS) account.

c. Totals may differ from the sum of the components due to rounding.

Figure 1 shows aggregate funding for the targeted accounts as a percentage of their FY2006 funding level, and illustrates how actual (FY2006-FY2012), requested (FY2007-FY2013), projected (FY2014-FY2017), and authorized appropriations (FY2008-FY2013) compare to different doubling rates using FY2006 as the base year. The thick black line at the top of the chart is at 200%, the doubling level. The data used in **Figure 1** is in current dollars, not constant dollars, therefore the effect of inflation on the purchasing power of these funds is not taken into consideration.

Figure 1. Doubling of Research Funding for Targeted Accounts: Appropriations and Authorizations Versus Selected Rates

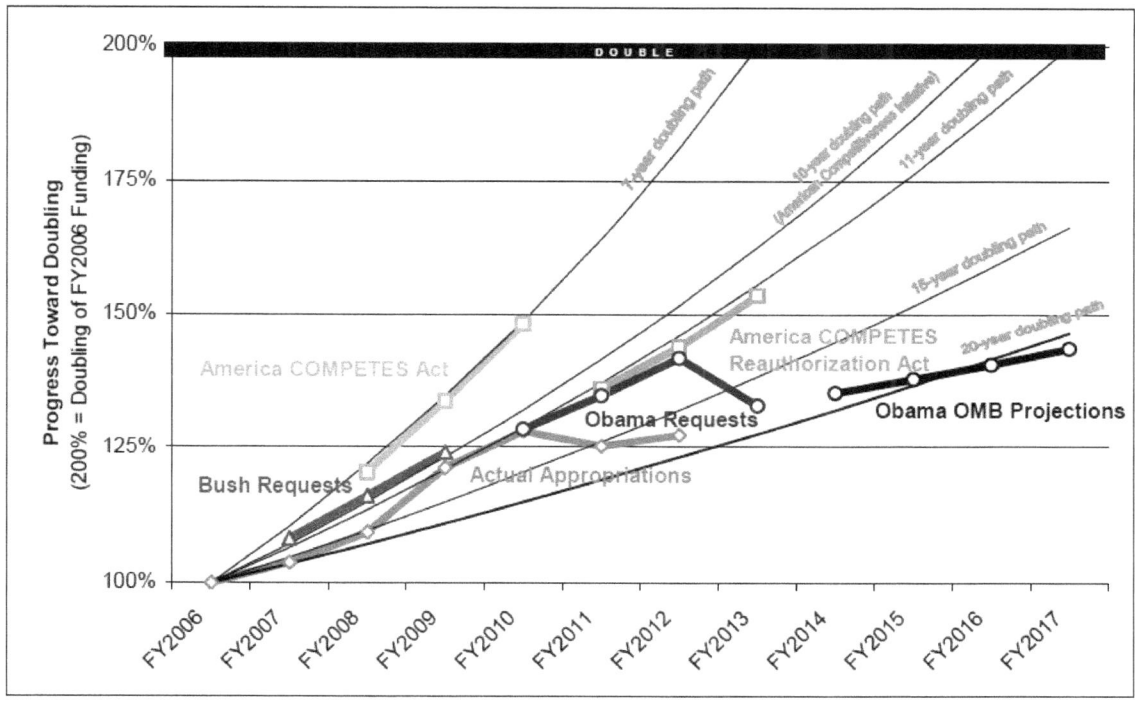

Source: Prepared by the Congressional Research Service (CRS) using agency budget justifications for fiscal years 2008, 2009, 2010, 2011, 2012, and 2013; the President's FY2013 budget request; and agency authorization levels from the America COMPETES Act (P.L. 110-69) and the America COMPETES Reauthorization Act of 2010 (P.L. 111-358).

Notes: The 7-year doubling pace represents annual increases of 10.4%, the 10-year doubling pace represents annual increases of 7.2%, the 11-year doubling pace represents annual increases of 6.5%, the 15-year doubling represents annual increases of 4.7%, and the 20-year doubling represents annual increases of 3.3%. Through compounding, these rates achieve the doubling of funding in the specified time period. The lines connecting aggregate appropriations for the targeted accounts are for illustration purposes only. With respect to "Actual Appropriations," aggregate data for FY2006-FY2012 is based on regular appropriations (funding provided under the American Recovery and Reinvestment Act of 2009 (P.L. 111-5) is not included). America COMPETES Act figures are based on aggregate funding for the target accounts as authorized by the act. America COMPETES Reauthorization Act of 2010 figures for FY2011-FY2013 are based on aggregate funding for the target accounts as authorized by the act.

National Nanotechnology Initiative

Funding for the National Nanotechnology Initiative (NNI) is requested in the amount of $1.766 billion for FY2013, $70 million (4.1%) above the FY2012 estimated level of $1.696 billion. Under the Administration's FY2013 request, nanotechnology funding would increase at the DOE by $127 million (40.3%), at the NSF by $9 million (2.1%), at the DOC by $7 million (7.0%), and at the EPA by $2 million (11.8%) over FY2012 funding levels. Nanotechnology funding for the DOD would fall by $72 million (-19.9%) under the 2013 request. Nanotechnology funding for other NNI agencies would remain essentially flat in FY2013.[24]

Networking and Information Technology Research and Development Program

President Obama has requested $3.807 billion in FY2013 funding for the Networking and Information Technology Research and Development (NITRD) program, $69 million (1.8%) above FY2012 funding. The NITRD request includes increases of $69 million (6.1%) for NSF, $33 million (5.9%) for DOE, $20 million (16.4%) for DOC, and $17 million (36.2%) for DHS. The President's budget would reduce DOD NITRD funding by $67 million (-5.7%). NITRD funding for other agencies would remain essentially flat in FY2013.[25]

U.S. Global Change Research Program

President Obama has proposed $2.563 billion for the U.S. Global Change Research Program (USGCRP) in FY2013, $136 million (5.6%) above the FY2012 estimated level of $2.427 billion. Four agencies would receive the bulk of the FY2013 USGCRP funding increase: NASA (up $79 million, 5.7%); DOC, including the National Oceanic and Atmospheric Administration and NIST (up $23 million, 7.2%); DOE (up $19 million, 9.0%), and the DOI (U.S. Geological Survey) ($9 million, 15.3%).[26]

Materials Genome Initiative

Announced in June 2011, the Materials Genome Initiative is a multi-agency initiative

> to create new knowledge, tools, and infrastructure with a goal of enabling U.S. industries to discover, manufacture, and deploy advanced materials twice as fast than is possible today. Agencies are currently developing implementation strategies for the Materials Genome Initiative with a focus on: (1) the creation of a materials innovation infrastructure, (2) achieving national goals with advanced materials, and (3) equipping the next generation

---

[24] Executive Office of the President, Office of Science and Technology Policy, *Science, Technology, Innovation, and STEM Education*, Table 2, February 13, 2011. For additional information on the NNI, see CRS Report RL34401, *The National Nanotechnology Initiative: Overview, Reauthorization, and Appropriations Issues*, by John F. Sargent Jr.

[25] Ibid.

[26] Executive Office of the President, Office of Science and Technology Policy, *Innovation, Education, and Infrastructure*, Table 2, February 14, 2011. For additional information on the USGCRP, see CRS Report RL33817, *Climate Change: Federal Program Funding and Tax Incentives*, by Jane A. Leggett.

materials workforce. Materials science funding opportunities announced in FY 2012 and requested in the FY 2013 Budget reflect these efforts.[27]

In Congressional testimony, OSTP Director John Holdren stated that the purpose of the Materials Genome Initiative is to "speed our understanding of the fundamentals of materials science, providing a wealth of practical information that American entrepreneurs and innovators will be able to use to develop new products and processes" in much the same way that the Human Genome Project accelerated a range of biological sciences by identifying and deciphering the human genetic code.[28]

Advanced Manufacturing Partnership

In June 2011, President Obama launched the Advanced Manufacturing Partnership (AMP), an effort to bring together "industry, universities, and the Federal government to invest in emerging technologies that will create high-quality manufacturing jobs and enhance our global competitiveness."[29] Two R&D-focused components of the AMP are the National Robotics Initiative (NRI) and the National Network for Manufacturing Innovation (NNMI). The President's FY2013 budget includes $2.2 billion for Federal advanced manufacturing R&D, a 19% increase over FY2012.[30]

National Robotics Initiative

The National Robotics Initiative (NRI) seeks to "develop robots that work with or beside people to extend or augment human capabilities."[31] Among the goals of the program are increasing labor productivity in the manufacturing sector, assisting with dangerous and expensive missions in space, accelerating the discovery of new drugs, and improving food safety by rapidly sensing microbial contamination.[32] In FY2012, four agencies—NSF, NIH, NASA, and USDA—issued a joint solicitation to provide research funding for next-generation robotics. In addition, the Department of Defense, through multiple component agencies, is supporting the NRI through the Defense University Research Instrumentation Program. DOD is supporting the purchase of equipment to assist in robotics research to advance defense technologies and applications, including unmanned ground, air, sea, and undersea vehicles and autonomous systems.[33]

---

[27] E-mail correspondence between OSTP and CRS, March 14, 2012.

[28] John P. Holdren, Director, Office of Science and Technology Policy, Executive Office of the President, testimony before the Senate Committee on Commerce, Science, and Transportation, Subcommittee on Science and Space, hearing on "Keeping America Competitive Through Investments in R&D," March 6, 2012, http://commerce.senate.gov/public/?a=Files.Serve&File_id=fed566eb-e2c8-49da-aec5-f84e4045890b.

[29] Ibid.

[30] Timothy F. Geithner, Secretary, U.S. Department of the Treasury, testimony before the House Committee on the Budget, hearing on "The President's Fiscal Year 2013 Revenue and Economic Policy Proposals," February 16, 2012, http://budget house.gov/UploadedFiles/GeithnerTestimony02162012.pdf.

[31] Ibid.

[32] Executive Office of the President, Office of Science and Technology Policy, website, August 3, 2011, http://www.whitehouse.gov/blog/2011/08/03/supporting-president-s-national-robotics-initiative.

[33] Ibid.

National Network for Manufacturing Innovation

The President's FY2013 budget also proposes establishment of a National Network for Manufacturing Innovation (NNMI) to promote the development of manufacturing technologies with broad applications. This initiative would be carried out through a collaboration between NIST, DOD, DOE, and NSF with mandatory funding of $1 billion.[34]

According to NIST, the NNMI would consist of

> a network of institutes where researchers, companies, and entrepreneurs can come together to develop new manufacturing technologies with broad applications. Each institute would have a unique technology focus. These institutes will help support an ecosystem of manufacturing activity in local areas. The Manufacturing Innovation Institutes would support manufacturing technology commercialization by helping to bridge the gap from the laboratory to the market and address core gaps in scaling manufacturing process technologies.[35]

The President's budget proposes mandatory spending of $1 billion over 10 years (FY2013-FY2022) in support of the NNMI, with initial funding of $206 million in FY2013. Funding for the program is front-loaded with $839 million in spending projected for FY2013-FY2017.[36]

FY2013 Appropriations Status

The remainder of this report provides a more in-depth analysis of R&D in 12 federal departments and agencies that, in aggregate, receive more than 98% of federal R&D funding. Annual appropriations for these agencies are provided through 8 of the 12 regular appropriations bills. As of June 1, 2012, one of the eight regular appropriations bills (Commerce, Justice, Science, and Related Agencies Appropriations Act, 2013) that provide R&D funding for agencies covered in-depth in this report had passed the House; none had passed the Senate. For each agency covered in this report, **Table 5** shows the corresponding regular appropriations bill that provides funding for the agency, including its R&D activities.

In addition to this report, CRS produces individual reports on each of the appropriations bills. These reports can be accessed via the CRS website at http://crs.gov/Pages/clis.aspx?cliid=73. Also, the status of each appropriations bill is available on the CRS webpage, *Status Table of Appropriations*, available at http://www.crs.gov/Pages/appover.aspx. This report will be updated as relevant appropriations bills are passed by the House or the Senate.

---

[34] According to OSTP, funding for the NNMI is mostly separate from the $2.2 billion proposed investment in advanced manufacturing under the AMP, though there is an overlap of $137 million. Email correspondence between OSTP and CRS, March 14, 2012.

[35] U.S. Department of Commerce, *FY2013 Budget in Brief*, February 2012, p. 123, http://www.osec.doc.gov/bmi/budget/FY13BIB/fy2013bib_final.pdf.

[36] Office of Management and Budget, Executive Office of the President, *Fiscal Year 2013 Budget of the U.S. Government*, February 2012, Table S-9, p. 217.

Table 5. Alignment of Agency R&D Funding and Regular Appropriations Bills

Department/Agency	Regular Appropriations Bill
Department of Defense	Department of Defense Appropriations Act
Department of Homeland Security	Department of Homeland Security Appropriations Act
National Institutes of Health	Departments of Labor, Health and Human Services, and Education, and Related Agencies Appropriations Act
Department of Energy	Energy and Water Development and Related Agencies Appropriations Act
National Science Foundation	Commerce, Justice, Science, and Related Agencies Appropriations Act
Department of Commerce National Institute of Standards and Technology National Oceanic and Atmospheric Administration	Commerce, Justice, Science, and Related Agencies Appropriations Act
National Aeronautics and Space Administration	Commerce, Justice, Science, and Related Agencies Appropriations Act
Department of Agriculture	Agriculture, Rural Development, Food and Drug Administration, and Related Agencies Appropriations Act
Department of the Interior	Department of the Interior, Environment, and Related Agencies Appropriations Act
Environmental Protection Agency	Department of the Interior, Environment, and Related Agencies Appropriations Act
Department of Transportation	Transportation, Housing and Urban Development, and Related Agencies Appropriations Act

Source: CRS website, FY2013 Status Table of Appropriations, available at http://www.crs.gov/Pages/appover.aspx.

Department of Defense[37]

Congress supports research and development in the Department of Defense (DOD) primarily through its Research, Development, Test, and Evaluation (RDT&E) appropriation. The appropriation supports the development of the nation's future military hardware and software and the technology base upon which those products rely.

Nearly all of what DOD spends on RDT&E is appropriated in Title IV of the defense appropriation bill. (See **Table 6**.) However, RDT&E funds are also appropriated in other parts of the bill. For example, RDT&E funds are appropriated as part of the Defense Health Program, the Chemical Agents and Munitions Destruction Program, and the National Defense Sealift Fund. The Defense Health Program supports the delivery of health care to DOD personnel and their families. Program funds are requested through the Operations and Maintenance appropriation. The program's RDT&E funds support congressionally directed research in such areas as breast, prostate, and ovarian cancer and other medical conditions. Congress appropriates funds for this program in Title VI (Other Department of Defense Programs) of the defense appropriations bill. The Chemical Agents and Munitions Destruction Program supports activities to destroy the U.S.

---

[37] This section was written by John Moteff, Specialist in Science and Technology Policy, CRS Resources, Science, and Industry Division.

inventory of lethal chemical agents and munitions to avoid future risks and costs associated with storage. Funds for this program have been requested through the Procurement appropriation. Congress appropriates funds for this program also in Title VI. The National Defense Sealift Fund supports the procurement, operation and maintenance, and research and development of the nation's naval reserve fleet and supports a U.S. flagged merchant fleet that can serve in time of need. Requests for this fund are made as part of the Navy's Procurement appropriation. Congress appropriates funds for this program in Title V (Revolving and Management Funds) of the defense appropriations bill.

The Joint Improvised Explosive Device Defeat Fund (JIEDDF) also contains RDT&E monies. However, the fund does not contain an RDT&E line item as do the three programs mentioned above. The Joint Improvised Explosive Device Defeat Office, which administers the fund, tracks (but does not report) the amount of funding allocated to RDT&E. The JIEDDF funding is not included in the table below.

RDT&E funds also have been requested and appropriated as part of DOD's separate funding to support efforts in what the Bush Administration had termed the Global War on Terror (GWOT), and what the Obama Administration refers to as Overseas Contingency Operations (OCO). Typically, the RDT&E funds appropriated for GWOT/OCO activities go to specified Program Elements (PEs) in Title IV. However, they are requested and accounted for separately. The Bush Administration requested these funds in separate GWOT emergency supplemental requests. The Obama Administration, while continuing to identify these funds uniquely as OCO requests, has included these funds as part of the regular budget, not in emergency supplementals. However, the Obama Administration will ask for additional OCO funds in supplemental requests, if the initial OCO funding is not enough to get through the fiscal year.

In addition, GWOT/OCO-related requests/appropriations often include money for a number of transfer funds. These have included in the past the Iraqi Freedom Fund (IFF), the Iraqi Security Forces Fund (which was not requested in FY2012), the Afghanistan Security Forces Fund, the Mine Resistant and Ambush Protected Vehicle Fund (MRAPVF), and the Pakistan Counterinsurgency Capability Fund (transferred to the State Department in FY2012). Congress typically makes a single appropriation into each of these funds, and authorizes the Secretary to make transfers to other accounts, including RDT&E, at his discretion. In the Consolidated Appropriations Act, 2012, Congress established a new Military Intelligence Program Transfer Fund, granting the Secretary similar authority.

For FY2013, the Obama Administration requested $69.408 billion for DOD's baseline Title IV RDT&E and another $246 million in OCO RDT&E. The FY2013 request is $2.902 billion and $280 million, respectively, below what Congress appropriated for FY2012. In addition, the Administration requested $673 million in RDT&E through the Defense Health Program, $647 million in RDT&E through the Chemical Agents and Munitions Destruction program, and $43 million in RDT&E through the National Defense Sealift Fund.

RDT&E funding can be analyzed in different ways. Each of the military departments request and receive their own RDT&E funding. So, too, do various DOD agencies (e.g., the Missile Defense Agency and the Defense Advanced Research Projects Agency), collectively aggregated within the Defensewide account. RDT&E funding also can be characterized by budget activity (i.e., the type of RDT&E supported). Those budget activities designated as 6.1, 6.2, and 6.3 (basic research, applied research, and advanced technology development, respectively) constitute what is called DOD's Science and Technology Program (S&T) and represent the more research-oriented part of the RDT&E program. Budget activities 6.4 and 6.5 focus on the development of specific weapon systems or components (e.g., the Joint Strike Fighter or missile defense systems), for which an operational need has been determined and an acquisition program established. Budget activity 6.6 provides management support, including support for test and evaluation facilities. Budget activity 6.7 supports system improvements in existing operational systems.

Many congressional policymakers are particularly interested in S&T funding since these funds support the development of new technologies and the underlying science. Some in the defense community see ensuring adequate support for S&T activities as imperative to maintaining U.S. military superiority. The knowledge generated at this stage of development can also contribute to advances in commercial technologies.

According to its FY2013 Budget Request Overview, DOD seeks to "maintain a strong S&T posture" going forward. The FY2013 Title IV baseline S&T funding request was $11.861 billion, $343 million less than what Congress appropriated for S&T in FY2012.

Within the S&T program, basic research (6.1) receives special attention, particularly by the nation's universities. DOD is not a large supporter of basic research, when compared to NIH or NSF. However, over half of DOD's basic research budget is spent at universities and represents the major contribution of funds in some areas of science and technology (such as electrical engineering and material science). The Administration requested $2.117 billion for basic research for FY2013, $5 million more than what Congress appropriated for Title IV basic research in FY2012.

Table 6. Department of Defense RDT&E

(in millions of dollars)

Budget Account	FY2011 Actual[a] Base + OCO	FY2012 Enacted[a] Base	OCO	FY2013 Request Base	OCO
Army	9,760	8,742	19	8,929	20
Navy	17,866	17,740	54	16,883	60
Air Force	27,421	26,480	260	25,428	53
Defensewide	20,895	19,161	194	17,982	112
Dir. Test & Eval.	192	188		185	
Total Title IV – By Account[b]	**76,135**	**72,310**	**526**	**69,408**	**246**
Budget Activity					
6.1 Basic Research	1,878	2,112		2,117	
6.2 Applied Research	4,329	4,739		4,478	
6.3 Advanced Dev.	5,340	5,353	59	5,266	
6.4 Advanced Component Dev. and Prototypes	14,142	13,450	12	12,409	24
6.5 Systems Dev. And Demo	14,346	14,129	11	14,695	2
6.6 Management Support[c]	5,661	4,566	18	4,263	5
6.7 Op. Systems Dev.[d]	30,441	27,960	427	26,180	214

Budget Account	FY2011 Actual[a]	FY2012 Enacted[a]		FY2013 Request	
	Base + OCO	Base	OCO	Base	OCO
Total Title IV—by Budget Activity[b]	76,135	72,310	526	69,408	246
Title V—Revolving and Management Funds					
National Defense Sealift Fund	18	48		43	
Title VI—Other Defense Programs					
Office of Inspector General	0	5		0	
Defense Health Program	1,206	1,267		673	
Chemical Agents and Munitions Destruction	393	497		647	
Grand Total[e]	77,752	74,127	526	70,771	246

Source: CRS, adapted from the Department of Defense Budget, Fiscal Year 2013 RDT&E Programs (R-1), February 2012 and relevant FY2013 Budget Justification (R-2) documents.

Notes:

a. Includes rescissions.

b. Total may differ from sum of components due to rounding.

c. Includes funding for the Director of Test and Evaluation.

d. Includes funding for classified programs.

e. The "Grand Total" figure uses the "Total Title IV – by Account" figure.

Department of Homeland Security[38]

For the Department of Homeland Security (DHS), the President has requested $1.179 billion for R&D and related programs in FY2013, a 20% increase from FY2012. This total includes $831 million for the Directorate of Science and Technology (S&T), $328 million for the Domestic Nuclear Detection Office (DNDO), and $20 million for Research, Development, Test, and Evaluation (RDT&E) in the U.S. Coast Guard. The House committee recommended a total of $1.162 billion, including $826 million for S&T, $316 million for DNDO, and $20 million for Coast Guard RDT&E. The Senate committee recommended the same amounts as the request. (See **Table 7**.)

The S&T Directorate is the primary DHS R&D organization.[39] Headed by the Under Secretary for Science and Technology, it performs R&D in several laboratories of its own and funds R&D performed by the DOE national laboratories, industry, universities, and others. The Administration has requested $831 million for the S&T Directorate for FY2013. This is 25%

---

[38] This section was written by Daniel Morgan, Specialist in Science and Technology Policy, CRS Resources, Science, and Industry Division.

[39] For more information, see CRS Report RL34356, *The DHS Directorate of Science and Technology: Key Issues for Congress*, by Dana A. Shea and Daniel Morgan.

more than the FY2012 appropriation of $668 million. Funding for Research, Development, and Innovation (RDI) would increase by $212 million. Of the six thrust areas within RDI, the largest requested increase (from $61 million in FY2012 to $144 million in FY2013) is for disaster resilience R&D. A reduction of $50 million in the request for Laboratory Facilities reflects the omission of funding for the National Bio and Agro-Defense Facility (NBAF), a planned replacement for the current Plum Island Animal Disease Center. The $50 million appropriated in FY2012 for the start of NBAF construction was one-third of what the Administration had requested. DHS has announced plans for an assessment of whether and for what purpose a facility like NBAF should be built. The assessment will consider current threats and will review cost, safety, and alternatives to the NBAF plan.

The House committee recommended $826 million for the S&T Directorate, or $6 million less than the request. The committee included $72 million less than the request for RDI and directed DHS to determine how to allocate that reduction across the six thrust areas. In Laboratory Facilities, the committee recommended $75 million more than the request and directed that it be spent on NBAF construction.

The Senate committee recommended S&T funding levels that were the same as the Administration's request. Within RDI, however, it specified separate amounts for each of the six thrust areas, rather than a single total. In recommending no funding for NBAF construction, the committee noted a total cost estimate for the facility of $1.138 billion.

The Domestic Nuclear Detection Office is the primary DHS organization for combating the threat of nuclear attack, responsible for all DHS nuclear detection research, development, testing, evaluation, acquisition, and operational support. The Administration has requested $328 million for DNDO for FY2013, an increase of 14% above the FY2012 appropriation of $289 million. The request includes an increase of $44 million for Transformational R&D. The Administration is no longer proposing to transfer this program to S&T. The increase for Transformational R&D is partially offset by a reduction of $23 million for Systems Development. In the Systems Acquisition account, funding for human-portable radiation detectors would increase by $20 million, while funding for radiation portal monitors would decrease to $1 million from $7 million in FY2012.

The House committee recommended $316 million for DNDO, or $12 million less than the request. Most of the recommended reduction was in the Transformational R&D program. The committee directed DHS to provide an updated implementation plan for its responsibilities under the domestic portion of the global nuclear detection architecture. It stated that it intends this to be annual report.

As for S&T, the Senate committee recommended DNDO funding levels that were the same as the Administration's request. Like the House committee, the Senate committee directed DHS to provide an updated implementation plan for its responsibilities under the domestic portion of the global nuclear detection architecture.

Table 7. Department of Homeland Security R&D and Related Programs

(in millions of dollars)

	FY2011 Enacteda	FY2012 Enacted	FY2013 Request	H.R. 5855 House Committee-reported	S. 3216 Senate Committee-reported
Directorate of Science and Technology	**$767**	**$668**	**$831**	**$826**	**$831**
Management and Administration	140	135	138	130	138
R&D, Acquisition, and Operations	626	533	693	696	693
Research, Development, and Innovation	—	*266*	*478*	*406*	*478*
Laboratory Facilities	*140*	*177*	*127*	*202*	*127*
Acquisition and Operations Support	—	*54*	*48*	*48*	*48*
University Programs	*40*	*37*	*40*	*40*	*40*
Other	*507*	—	—	—	—
Rescission of Prior-Year Unobligated Balances	*(61)*	—	—	—	—
Domestic Nuclear Detection Office	**331**	**289**	**328**	**316**	**328**
Management and Administration	37	37	40	38	40
Research, Development, and Operations	264	215	237	227	237
Systems Engineering and Architecture	*33*	*30*	*30*	*30*	*30*
Systems Development	*53*	*51*	*28*	*28*	*28*
Transformational R&D	*96*	*40*	*84*	*75*	*84*
Assessments	*38*	*38*	*33*	*33*	*33*
Operations Support	*33*	*33*	*36*	*36*	*36*
National Technical Nuclear Forensics Center	*22*	*23*	*26*	*26*	*26*
Rescission of Prior-Year Unobligated Balances	*(11)*	—	—	—	—
Systems Acquisition	30	37	51	51	51
Radiation Portal Monitors Program	—	*7*	*1*	*1*	*1*
Securing the Cities	*20*	*22*	*22*	*22*	*22*
Human Portable Radiation Detection Systems	*10*	*8*	*28*	*28*	*28*
U.S. Coast Guard RDT&E	**25**	**28**	**20**	**20**	**20**
TOTAL	**1,122**	**984**	**1,179**	**1,162**	**1,179**

Source: FY2011 from P.L. 112-10 and DHS FY2011 expenditure plan dated June 17, 2011. FY2012 from P.L. 112-74 and H.Rept. 112-331. FY2013 request from DHS FY2013 congressional budget justification, http://www.dhs.gov/xabout/budget/dhs-budget.shtm. FY2013 House Committee from H.R. 5855 as reported and H.Rept. 112-492. FY2013 Senate Committee from S. 3216 and S.Rept. 112-169.

Note: Amounts within the S&T Directorate's R&D, Acquisition, and Operations account were categorized differently in FY2011.

a. Includes rescissions.

National Institutes of Health[40]

The FY2013 President's Budget requests a program level total of $30.860 billion for NIH, which is the same as the FY2012 level and $65 million lower than the comparable FY2011 amount of $30.926 billion (see **Table 8**). The final FY2012 total dropped below the FY2011 level after adjustment for the rescissions mandated in the Consolidated Appropriations Act, 2012 (P.L. 112-74), and a separate transfer of funds within HHS.[41]

NIH Organization and Sources of Funding. NIH supports and conducts a wide range of basic and clinical research, research training, and health information dissemination across all fields of biomedical and behavioral sciences. About 83% of NIH's budget goes out to the extramural research community in the form of grants, contracts, and other awards. The funding supports research performed by more than 300,000 non-federal scientists and technical personnel who work at more than 2,500 universities, hospitals, medical schools, and other research institutions around the country and abroad. The agency's organization consists of the Office of the NIH Director and 27 institutes and centers. The Office of the Director (OD) sets overall policy for NIH and coordinates the programs and activities of all NIH components, particularly in areas of research that involve multiple institutes. The institutes and centers (collectively called ICs) focus on particular diseases, areas of human health and development, or aspects of research support. Each IC plans and manages its own research programs in coordination with the Office of the Director. As shown in **Table 8**, Congress provides a separate appropriation to 24 of the 27 ICs, to OD, and to an intramural Buildings and Facilities account. (The other three centers, not included in the table, are funded through the NIH Management Fund.)

Funding for NIH comes primarily from the annual appropriations bill for the Departments of Labor, Health and Human Services, and Education, and Related Agencies (Labor/HHS), with an additional amount for Superfund-related activities from the appropriations bill for the Department of the Interior, Environment, and Related Agencies (Interior/Environment). Those two bills provide NIH's discretionary budget authority. In addition, NIH receives mandatory funding of $150 million annually that is provided in the Public Health Service (PHS) Act for a special program on type 1 diabetes research, and also receives $8.2 million annually for the National Library of Medicine from a transfer within PHS. Until FY2012, Congress had for the previous 10 years provided that a portion of NIH's Labor/HHS appropriation be transferred to the Global Fund to Fight HIV/AIDS, Tuberculosis, and Malaria. The transfer—in recent years about $300 million—was part of the U.S. contribution to the Global Fund. The total funding available for NIH activities, taking account of add-ons and transfers, is the program level. Because the "NIH program level" cited in the Administration's FY2013 budget documents does not reflect the transfer-out of the Global Fund money in FY2011, **Table 8** shows the program level both before and after the transfer. Congress terminated the transfer in FY2012.

NIH and other HHS agencies and programs that are authorized under the PHS Act are subject to a budget tap called the PHS Program Evaluation Set-Aside. Section 241 of the PHS Act (42 U.S.C. §238j) authorizes the Secretary to use a portion of eligible appropriations to assess the

---

[40] This section was written by Pamela W. Smith, Analyst in Biomedical Policy, CRS Domestic Social Policy Division. For further information on NIH, see CRS Report R41705, *The National Institutes of Health (NIH): Organization, Funding, and Congressional Issues*, by Judith A. Johnson and Pamela W. Smith.

[41] FY2011 funding was provided in P.L. 112-10, The Department of Defense and Full-Year Continuing Appropriations Act, 2011.

effectiveness of federal health programs and to identify ways to improve them. Congress sets the percentage level of the tap in the annual Labor/HHS appropriations acts, and also directs specific amounts of funding from the tap to a number of HHS programs. The set-aside has the effect of redistributing appropriated funds for specific purposes among PHS and other HHS agencies. NIH, with the largest budget among the PHS agencies, becomes the largest "donor" of program evaluation funds, and is a relatively minor recipient. Section 205 of the FY2012 Labor/HHS appropriations act capped the set-aside at 2.5%, which drew over $700 million from the NIH budget. The FY2013 President's Budget proposes to increase the set-aside to 3.2%, which might increase the NIH contribution by about $200 million. By convention, budget tables such as **Table 8** do not subtract the amount of the evaluation tap, or of other taps within HHS, from the agencies' appropriations.[42]

FY2013 President's Budget Request. Most of the institutes and centers are essentially flat-funded in the request, with a few specific increases and decreases noted below. NIH describes its areas of emphasis for FY2013 under four broad themes that build on its current activities and continue the implementation of an organizational restructuring for translational medicine that started in FY2012.

Investing in Basic Research. Congress has given NIH strong direction to continue its emphasis on support of basic biomedical and behavioral research, which seeks to understand the causes of disease onset and progression. About 54% of the proposed FY2013 budget would be spent on basic research in areas such as genetics, biological processes involving proteins and metabolic pathways, stem cells and regenerative medicine, and environmental and behavioral influences on health.

Accelerating Discovery Through Technology. NIH would continue to support development and application of advanced technologies (such as DNA sequencing, microarray technology, nanotechnology, new imaging modalities, and computational biology) to increase understanding of complex diseases and enable development of more effective therapies. One of NIH's high-priority projects is The Cancer Genome Atlas (TCGA), which will generate maps of the key genetic changes found in different types of cancer.

Advancing Translational Sciences. Translational medicine focuses on converting basic research discoveries into clinical applications that benefit patients. Starting in 2010, NIH began planning for creation of a new National Center for Advancing Translational Sciences (NCATS). The new entity would pull into one place a variety of preclinical and clinical translational sciences capabilities and programs that were scattered across other institutes and centers. Congress established and funded NCATS in the FY2012 appropriations act; it also abolished the National Center for Research Resources and transferred its programs to NCATS and several other ICs. The NCATS mission includes exploring more reliable, rapid, and cost-effective ways to test possible new drugs, diagnostics, and preventive measures for human use (or new uses for old products). In addition, NCATS is to foster partnerships between extramural researchers, industry, and health care and government entities to speed commercialization of new therapies and allow for rapid dissemination and adoption of new treatments.[43]

---

[42] For further information on the PHS Evaluation Set-Aside, see CRS Report R41737, *Public Health Service (PHS) Agencies: Overview and Funding, FY2010-FY2012*, coordinated by C. Stephen Redhead and Pamela W. Smith.

[43] See National Institutes of Health, "NIH Establishes National Center for Advancing Translational Sciences," press release, December 23, 2011, http://www.nih.gov/news/health/dec2011/od-23.htm.

The FY2013 budget request for NCATS is $639 million, an increase of $64 million (11%) over its FY2012 first-year budget. Nearly $40 million of the increase would go to expanding the Cures Acceleration Network (CAN) from $10 million to almost $50 million. An example of NIH's use of CAN's flexible award authority is support of the Integrated Microsystems for Drug Screening Initiative, a collaboration between NIH, the Food and Drug Administration, and the Defense Advanced Research Projects Agency to develop a chip composed of human cells and tissues that can be used to rapidly screen for safe and effective drugs. The initiative previously received funding from the NIH Common Fund. The large Clinical and Translational Science Awards (CTSA) program, which funds a national consortium of medical research institutions engaged in improving clinical research, would receive a $1 million increase to $463 million.

Encouraging New Investigators and New Ideas. NIH has several programs to support exceptional young scientists and speed their transition to independent research. Funded from the High-Risk Research program of the NIH Common Fund, the NIH Director's New Innovator Award program provides first-time independent awards to outstanding investigators; the Administration requests $80 million to support these awards in FY2013, the same as in FY2012. The NIH Director's Early Independence Program supports talented junior scientists, allowing them to by-pass the traditional postdoctoral training period and move directly to an independent research career; the President requests $12 million for this program, up from $8 million in FY2012. For NIH's major research training program, the Ruth L. Kirschstein National Research Service Awards, the budget proposes funding of $775 million, $2 million below FY2012. That level would support a 2% stipend increase and 16,361 training positions, a decrease of 309 positions. NIH is also systematically analyzing biomedical workforce and training needs, with a special focus on promoting diversity in the workforce and understanding barriers to career advancement.

Selected Other Program Changes in IC Budgets. *Institutional Development Awards (IDeA):* Last year, the FY2012 appropriation provided the IDeA program with a $50 million increase (22%) to $276 million, and NIH was encouraged to broaden the eligibility criteria for these research capacity and infrastructure grants. For FY2013, the Administration has not requested continuation of the extra funding—the budget request for the National Institute of General Medical Sciences includes $225 million for the IDeA program, $51 million less than in FY2012.

National Children's Study: The budget request for the Office of the Director is $28 million below FY2012 because funding for the National Children's Study would drop by nearly 15% from $193 million to $165 million. The pilot Vanguard Study is moving to a less resource-intensive phase, and NIH says it is evaluating more cost-effective sampling approaches for the whole study.

Alzheimer's disease research: In February 2012, the Administration announced that NIH would be devoting additional resources to Alzheimer's disease research in both FY2012 and FY2013.[44] Within FY2012 appropriations, NIH planned to redirect $50 million from other research areas to Alzheimer's-related grants. In FY2013, HHS plans to make available $80 million from the Prevention and Public Health Fund (mandatory funding provided by the Affordable Care Act) for a portfolio of new research on Alzheimer's. The proposal could prove contentious in light of current debates over the use of the Prevention Fund.

---

[44] U.S. Department of Health and Human Services, "We Can't Wait: Administration Announces New Steps to Fight Alzheimer's Disease," press release, February 7, 2012, http://www.hhs.gov/news/press/2012pres/02/20120207a.html.

Research Project Grants. The main funding mechanism for supporting extramural investigator-initiated research is competitive, peer-reviewed research project grants (RPGs). The FY2013 President's Budget requests total funding for RPGs of $16.5 billion, representing about 52% of NIH's proposed budget. The amount is a decrease of $26 million (-0.2%) from the FY2012 level. The request would support an estimated 35,888 RPG awards, 56 fewer grants than in FY2012. Within that total, 9,415 would be competing RPGs, 672 (7.7%) more than in FY2012. ("Competing" awards means new grants plus competing renewals of existing grants.) The average cost of a competing RPG in FY2013 is estimated to be about $431,000, up from about $423,000 in FY2012. The increase is due to the cycling of the high-cost HIV/AIDS Clinical Trials Networks grants into competing status in FY2013. After adjusting for those large grants, there is an overall reduction of 1% in the average cost of competing RPGs.

NIH has proposed several grant-funding policies in order to maximize resources for investigator-initiated grants and for young, first-time researchers. Non-competing (continuation) RPGs would have their budgets reduced by 1% from the FY2012 level, and the budgets of competing RPGs would be negotiated downward by about 1% to avoid growth in the average award size. NIH would continue current policies that equalize the success rates of new and established investigators in receiving funding. Additional review and scrutiny is planned for awards to any scientist who already has total grant support of $1.5 million or more.

Other Funding Mechanisms. The FY2013 request also proposed changes for other funding mechanisms within the NIH budget besides those for RPGs and training awards. Support for *research centers* would decrease by $64 million (-2.1%) to $2.966 billion, largely because of the $51 million drop in funding for the IDeA program mentioned previously. The catch-all *R&D contracts* mechanism is proposed for a $108 million (3.6%) increase to $3.076 billion, reflecting (among other things) funding to cover the proposed increase in the PHS Program Evaluation Set-Aside. The NIH *intramural research program* would gain $21 million (0.6%) for a total of $3.420 billion. *Research management and support* has a requested increase of $1.7 million (0.1%) to a total of $1.535 billion. The appropriation for the *Office of the Director* would decrease by $28 million to $1.429 billion because of the plans for the National Children's Study discussed earlier. Also funded through the OD account is the NIH Common Fund, which supports research in emerging areas of scientific opportunity, public health challenges, or knowledge gaps that might benefit from collaboration between two or more institutes or centers. The request for the Common Fund is $545 million, the same as the FY2012 level. The appropriation for *Buildings and Facilities* is $125 million, the same as FY2012.

Table 8. National Institutes of Health Funding

(in millions of dollars)

Component	FY2011 Comparable[a]	FY2012 Comparable[b]	FY2013 Request
Cancer (NCI)	5,050	5,066	5,069
Heart/Lung/Blood (NHLBI)	3,065	3,075	3,076
Dental/Craniofacial Research (NIDCR)	409	410	408
Diabetes/Digestive/Kidney (NIDDK)	1,789	1,795	1,792
Neurological Disorders/Stroke (NINDS)	1,619	1,624	1,625
Allergy/Infectious Diseases (NIAID)[c]	4,768	4,485	4,495
General Medical Sciences (NIGMS)	2,368	2,427	2,379

Component	FY2011 Comparable[a]	FY2012 Comparable[b]	FY2013 Request
Child Health/Human Development (NICHD)	1,316	1,320	1,321
Eye (NEI)	700	702	693
Environmental Health Sciences (NIEHS)	683	685	684
Aging (NIA)	1,099	1,102	1,103
Arthritis/Musculoskeletal/Skin (NIAMS)	533	535	536
Deafness/Communication Disorders (NIDCD)	414	416	417
Nursing Research (NINR)	144	145	144
Alcohol Abuse/Alcoholism (NIAAA)	458	459	457
Drug Abuse (NIDA)	1,049	1,052	1,054
Mental Health (NIMH)	1,475	1,479	1,479
Human Genome Research (NHGRI)	511	512	511
Biomedical Imaging/Bioengineering (NIBIB)	345	338	337
Complementary/Alternative Medicine (NCCAM)	127	128	128
Minority Health/Health Disparities (NIMHD)	276	276	279
Fogarty International Center (FIC)	69	70	70
Center for Advancing Translational Sciences (NCATS)	554	575	639
National Library of Medicine (NLM)	362	365	373
Office of Director (OD)	1,454	1,457	1,429
Common Fund	*543*	*545*	*545*
Buildings & Facilities (B&F)	50	125	125
Subtotal, Labor/HHS Appropriation	30,688	30,623	30,623
Superfund (Interior appropriation to NIEHS)[d]	79	79	79
Total, NIH discretionary budget authority	30,767	30,702	30,702
Pre-appropriated type 1 diabetes funds[e]	150	150	150
PHS Evaluation Tap funding[f]	8	8	8
Total, NIH program level	30,926	30,860	30,860
Total, NIH program level (less Global Fund)	30,628	30,860	30,860

Source: Adapted by CRS from National Institutes of Health, *Justification of Estimates for Appropriations Committees, FY2013*, Vol. 1 - Overview/Supplementary Tables, February 13, 2012, p. ST-2, http://officeofbudget.od.nih.gov/pdfs/FY13/Vol%201%20Tab%203%20-%20Supplementary%20Tables.pdf. Details may not add to totals due to rounding.

a. FY2011 figures are shown on a comparable basis to FY2012 and FY2013, reflecting the NCATS reorganization in FY2012 and including the Global AIDS Fund transfer amount of $297.3 million. The FY2011 level reflects real transfer of $998 thousand from HHS/Office of the Secretary to NIMH.

b. The Consolidated Appropriations Act, 2012 (H.R. 2055, P.L. 112-74), enacted December 23, 2011, included nine regular FY2012 appropriations bills. NIH appropriations were provided in Division F (Labor/HHS/ Education) and Division E (Interior/Environment). Amounts shown reflect across-the-board rescissions of 0.189% (Division F) and 0.16% (Division E), Secretary's transfer of $8.727 million to Health Resources and Services Administration, and comparable transfers from ICs to NLM. Reflects the termination of the Global AIDS transfer in FY2012.

c.   The FY2011 amount includes $297.3 million for transfer to the Global Fund for HIV/AIDS, Tuberculosis, and Malaria. Congress terminated the Global Fund transfer in FY2012.

d.   Separate account in the Interior/Environment appropriations for NIEHS research activities related to Superfund.

e.   Mandatory funds available to NIDDK for type I diabetes research under PHS Act §330B (provided by P.L. 110-275 and P.L. 111-309). Funds have been appropriated through FY2013.

f.   Additional funds for NLM from PHS Evaluation Set-Aside (§241 of PHS Act).

Department of Energy[45]

The Administration has requested $12.763 billion for Department of Energy (DOE) R&D and related programs in FY2013, including activities in three major categories: science, national security, and energy. This request is 8.2% more than the FY2012 appropriation of $11.794 billion. The House committee recommended $11.705 billion. The Senate committee recommended $12.240 billion. (See **Table 9** for details.)

The request for the DOE Office of Science is $4.992 billion, an increase of 2.4% from the FY2012 appropriation of $4.874 billion. The Administration's stated goal is to double the funding of the Office of Science.[46] This continues a plan initiated by the Bush Administration in January 2006. The original target under both Administrations was to achieve the doubling goal in the decade from FY2006 to FY2016. The current policy no longer specifies a completion date. The FY2013 request is 37% more than the FY2006 baseline. The America COMPETES Reauthorization Act of 2010 (P.L. 111-358) authorizes $6.007 billion for the Office of Science in FY2013. The House and Senate committee recommendations were $4.801 billion and $4.909 billion respectively.

The Office of Science includes six major research programs. A requested increase of $112 million for the largest program, basic energy sciences (BES), would fund "new science supporting a clean energy agenda," materials and chemistry by design, and joint R&D with the Office of Energy Efficiency and Renewable Energy (EERE). Costs for increased utilization of existing BES facilities and the start of construction of the Linac Coherent Light Source-II, a high-energy x-ray source, would be mostly offset by a scheduled ramp-down in construction for the National Synchrotron Light Source-II. The House committee recommended $142 million less than the request for BES. The Senate committee recommended $88 million less than the request. Both committees rejected the proposal for BES energy frontier research centers to work jointly with EERE. In the fusion energy sciences program, the request would increase the U.S. contribution to the International Thermonuclear Experimental Reactor (ITER) by $45 million, but this would be more than offset by reduced funding for domestic fusion activities. In particular, the Alcator C-Mod tokamak, a fusion reactor, would cease operations. The estimated total cost for the U.S. share of ITER, a multi-year construction project, remains in the range of $1.45 billion to $2.2 billion, but "it is possible that costs will increase."[47] The House committee recommended $76 million more than the request for fusion, including domestic funding at the FY2012 level and $28

---

[45] This section was written by Daniel Morgan, Specialist in Science and Technology Policy, CRS Resources, Science, and Industry Division.

[46] For more information, see CRS Report R41951, *An Analysis of Efforts to Double Federal Funding for Physical Sciences and Engineering Research*, by John F. Sargent Jr.

[47] DOE FY2013 congressional budget justification, vol. 4, p. 191.

million more than requested for ITER. The Senate committee's recommendation for fusion was the same as the request.

The request for DOE national security R&D is $4.054 billion, an 8.1% increase from $3.752 billion in FY2012. The request for nonproliferation and verification R&D includes a one-time increment of $150 million for domestic uranium enrichment R&D and demonstration. The House committee agreed to the proposed increment for domestic uranium enrichment; the Senate committee rejected it.

The request for DOE energy R&D is $3.717 billion, up 17.3% from $3.168 billion in FY2012. In energy efficiency, funding for the Advanced Manufacturing Office (formerly the Industrial Technologies Program) would increase by $174 million, and funding for building technologies and vehicle technologies would increase by $91 million each. In renewable energy, funding for biomass and biorefinery systems would increase by $71 million, while funding for water power and for hydrogen and fuel cell technologies would decrease. A proposed increase in funding for fossil energy R&D reflects the rescission of unobligated prior-year balances in FY2012; excluding this rescission, the FY2013 request for fossil energy R&D is a decrease of $105 million, mostly from the coal program. The request for the Advanced Research Projects Agency–Energy (ARPA-E) is $350 million, an increase of $75 million. The House and Senate committees both provided less than the request for energy efficiency, renewable energy, and ARPA-E, and more than the request for fossil energy.

Table 9. Department of Energy R&D and Related Programs

(in millions of dollars)

	FY2011 Enacted[a]	FY2012 Enacted	FY2013 Request	H.R. 5325 House Committee-reported	S. 2465 Senate Committee-reported
Science	**$4,843**	**$4,874**	**$4,992**	**$4,801**	**$4,909**
Basic Energy Sciences	1,678	1,688	1,800	1,657	1,712
High Energy Physics	795	791	777	777	782
Biological and Environmental Research	612	610	625	542	625
Nuclear Physics	540	547	527	548	540
Advanced Scientific Computing Research	422	441	456	442	456
Fusion Energy Sciences	375	401	398	475	398
Other	420	396	410	361	396
National Security	**3,708**	**3,752**	**4,054**	**4,006**	**3,952**
Weapons Activities[b]	2,369	2,307	2,398	2,381	2,426
Naval Reactors	959	1,080	1,089	1,087	1,089
Nonproliferation and Verification R&D	361	354	548	528	418
Defense Environmental Cleanup Tech. Devt.	19	11	20	10	20
Energy	**3,019**	**3,168**	**3,717**	**2,898**	**3,378**
Energy Efficiency and Renewable Energy[c]	1,564	1,682	2,072	1,295	1,717
Fossil Energy R&D	445	347	421	554	461

	FY2011 Enacted[a]	FY2012 Enacted	FY2013 Request	H.R. 5325 House Committee-reported	S. 2465 Senate Committee-reported
Nuclear Energy	726	765	770	765	785
Electricity Delivery & Energy Reliability R&D	105	99	103	83	103
Advanced Research Projects Agency–Energy	180	275	350	200	312
Total	**11,570**	**11,794**	**12,763**	**11,705**	**12,240**

Source: FY2011 from P.L. 112-10 and H.Rept. 112-118. FY2012 and FY2013 request from DOE FY2013 congressional budget justification, http://www.cfo.doe.gov/budget/13budget/index13.html. FY2013 House Committee from H.R. 5325 as reported and H.Rept. 112-462. FY2013 Senate committee from S. 2465 as reported and S.Rept. 112-164.

Notes: Totals may differ from the sum of their components due to rounding. All amounts are reduced for rescissions and use of prior-year balances. FY2012 amounts are reduced to reflect allocation of the contractor pay freeze rescission in Sec. 309 of P.L. 112-74.

a. Includes rescissions.

b. Including Stockpile Services R&D Support, Stockpile Services R&D Certification and Safety, Science, Engineering except Enhanced Surety and Enhanced Surveillance, Inertial Confinement Fusion, Advanced Simulation and Computing, National Security Applications, and prorated shares of Readiness in Technical Base and Facilities and Legacy Contractor Pensions. Additional R&D activities may take place in the subprograms of Directed Stockpile Work that are devoted to specific weapon systems, but these funds are not included in the table because detailed funding schedules for those subprograms are classified.

c. Excluding Weatherization and Intergovernmental Activities.

National Science Foundation[48]

The National Science Foundation (NSF) supports basic research and education in the non-medical sciences and engineering. Congress established the Foundation as an independent federal agency in 1950 and directed it to "promote the progress of science; to advance the national health, prosperity, and welfare; to secure the national defense; and for other purposes."[49] The NSF is a primary source of federal support for U.S. university research, especially in certain fields such as mathematics and computer science. It is also responsible for significant shares of the federal science, technology, engineering, and mathematics (STEM) education program portfolio and federal STEM student aid and support.

The President requests a total of $7.373 billion in funding for NSF in FY2013. This amount is $340.0 million (4.8%) more than the Foundation's FY2012 estimated funding level of $7.033 billion and $926.9 million (-11.2%) less than the America COMPETES Reauthorization Act of 2010 (P.L. 111-358) authorized level of $8.300 billion. The House-passed top line for the NSF is $7.333 billion. This amount is $40.6 million (-0.6%) less than the request, $299.4 million (4.3%) more than the FY2012 estimate, and $59.4 million (0.8%) more than the $7.273 billion recommended by the Senate Committee on Appropriations.

---

[48] This section was written by Heather B. Gonzalez, Specialist in Science and Technology Policy, CRS Resources, Science, and Industry Division. Numbers are rounded. Data available upon request.

[49] The National Science Foundation Act of 1950 (P.L. 81-507).

Since FY2006, increases in the NSF budget have been at least partially driven by the so-called "doubling path policy." Congress and successive Administrations sought to double funding for the NSF, Department of Energy's Office of Science, and National Institute of Standards and Technology's core laboratory and construction accounts (collectively "the targeted accounts").[50] Under current authorizations for FY2011 to FY2013, targeted account funding levels would have increased at a compound annual growth rate of 6.3%, a pace that would result in doubling in approximately 11 years.[51] However, appropriations in FY2011 and FY2012 for the targeted accounts increased at rates of 4.6% and 4.1%, respectively (about an 18-year doubling pace). The President's FY 2013 budget request establishes a 4.1% compound annual growth rate for targeted accounts. This pace is similar to the 4.1% growth rate set by the FY2012 enacted appropriations, but lower than the authorized rate. Some legislators have raised concerns about pursuing the doubling effort given the nation's current fiscal challenges, including one who urged observers "to be realistic about the notion of doubling the NSF budget" in FY2013.[52] House and Senate proposals for targeted accounts in FY2013 would establish about a 20-year doubling pace.

The full House and Senate Committee on Appropriations agree on essentially identical appropriations levels for five of NSF's six major accounts in FY2013. (See **Table 10**.)[53] The primary difference between the two proposals is in the main research account (Research and Related Activities or R&RA). The House would provide $59.4 million (1.0%) more to the R&RA account in FY2013.[54]

The President's FY2013 request for R&RA is $5.983 billion, $294.3 million (5.2%) more than the FY2012 estimated level of $5.689 billion, and $654.5 million (-9.9%) less than the America COMPETES Reauthorization Act of 2010 (P.L. 111-358) authorized level of $6.638 billion. NSF's budget request highlights priorities in interdisciplinary research, clean energy, advanced manufacturing, materials, wireless communications, smart systems, and cybersecurity. The FY2013 R&RA request includes increases for all but one of the research directorates.[55] The largest requested R&RA increase (by amount and percentage) is for the Integrative Activities (IA) account. Increases in IA would largely apply to the R&RA contribution to the Graduate Research Fellowship (GRF) program[56] and to increased support for the Integrated NSF Support Promoting

---

[50] For an analysis of the doubling effort that includes historic trends, see CRS Report R41951, *An Analysis of Efforts to Double Federal Funding for Physical Sciences and Engineering Research*, by John F. Sargent Jr.

[51] As authorized by the America COMPETES Reauthorization Act of 2010 (P.L. 111-358).

[52] Opening Statement of Ranking Member Dan Lipinski, in U.S. Congress, House Committee on Science, Space, and Technology, Subcommittee on Research and Science Education, "The National Science Foundation's FY2013 Budget Request," hearings, 112th Cong., 2nd sess., February 28, 2012, http://democrats.science house.gov/sites/democrats.science house.gov/files/documents/DWL%20Opening%20Statement%20NSF%20FY13%20Budget.pdf.

[53] Funds from major NSF accounts may be merged at the program level and in many cases NSF's education, facilities, and research activities are deeply integrated as a matter of practice.

[54] R&RA is the primary source of research funding at the NSF and the largest account at the Foundation. Between FY2003 and FY2012, R&RA's share of the NSF budget increased by 3.7%. This increase appears to be attributable, at least in part, to more rapid budget growth in the R&RA account than in other NSF accounts. Between FY2003 actual and the FY2012 estimate the total NSF budget grew by $1.664 billion. 92.9% of this increase ($1.545 billion) went to R&RA. By comparison, the average role for R&RA in the total NSF budget during this period was 79.5%. For more information on historical funding trends at NSF, see CRS Report R42470, *An Analysis of STEM Education Funding at the NSF: Trends and Policy Discussion*, by Heather B. Gonzalez.

[55] Increases for the R&RA directorates range from 2.1% for Social, Behavioral, and Economic Sciences to 23.4% for Integrative Activities. The only reduction in the request is to the U.S. Arctic Research Commission, for which NSF seeks a $60,000 (4.1%) reduction from the FY2012 estimate of $1.45 million.

[56] The FY2013 IA request for the GRF is $121.5 million, which is $33.0 million (37.3%) more than the FY2012 (continued...)

Interdisciplinary Research and Education (INSPIRE) program.[57] NSF also seeks an increase in the Innovation Corps (I-Corps) program.[58]

The House proposes $5.943 billion for R&RA in FY2013. This amount is $59.4 million (0.1%) more than the Senate Committee on Appropriations' recommendation, $40.6 million (0.7%) less than the FY2013 request, and $253.7 million (4.5%) more than the FY2012 estimate. H.Rept. 112-463, which accompanied H.R. 5326 (Commerce, Justice, Science, and Related Agencies Appropriations Act, 2013) when it left the House Appropriations Committee, directs NSF to prioritize—of new R&RA activities—cybersecurity, advanced manufacturing, materials, and research in the natural and physical sciences, math, and engineering. In particular, the House report provides the requested level of $148.9 million for NSF's Advanced Manufacturing initiative. Other R&RA provisions in the House report include a requirement that I-Corps recipients commit to the domestic production of goods or services commercialized with NSF assistance; two required reports on the management of scientific facilities; and language encouraging NSF to establish neuroscience as a cross-cutting theme. H.Rept. 112-463 also endorses NSF-proposed changes in R&RA; except for the proposed termination of the Communicating Science Broadly program, which the House Committee on Appropriations seeks to maintain.

The Senate Committee on Appropriations recommends $5.883 billion for R&RA in FY2013. This amount is $100.0 million (-1.7%) less than the President's request and $194.3 million (3.4%) more than the FY2012 estimate of $5.689 billion. Among other things, S.Rept. 112-158 highlights R&RA support for scientific facilities and instrumentation; provides the requested levels for astronomical sciences ($244.6 million) and cybersecurity research ($161.0 million); and expresses concerns about the adequacy of funding levels for the Academic Research Fleet. The Senate committee report also provides the requested level of funding ($7.5 million) for Large Synoptic Survey Telescope pre-construction planning. Other R&RA provisions in S.Rept. 112-158 include $158.0 million for the Experimental Program to Stimulate Competitive Research (EPSCoR) in FY2013. This amount is slightly below the President's FY2013 request for $158.2 million and is $7.1 million (4.7%) more than the FY2012 estimate of $150.9 million.

Other accounts that fund R&D at the NSF include the Education and Human Resources (E&HR) account and Major Research Equipment and Facilities Construction (MREFC). For E&HR, the President requests $875.6 million in FY2013. This amount is $46.6 million (5.6%) more than the FY2012 estimated level of $829.0 million and $166.2 million (-16.0%) less than the America COMPETES Reauthorization Act of 2010 (P.L. 111-358) authorized level of $1.042 billion. The FY2013 budget request for E&HR reframes NSF education programs—emphasizing core R&D activities, scholarships, and partnerships with research directorates and other federal agencies. The President's request seeks $20.0 million in new funding ($5.0 million for each division) to establish the reframing effort.[59] The FY2013 request also seeks funding for a new NSF-wide

---

(...continued)

estimated level of $88.5 million. The FY2013 NSF-wide request for GRF is $243.0 million, which is $45.0 million (22.7%) over the FY2012 estimate of $198.4 million. GRF is co-funded roughly equally by R&RA and E&HR.

[57] The FY2013 IA request for INSPIRE is $31.0 million, $18.7 million (151.0%) more than the FY2012 estimated level of $12.4 million. The NSF-wide request for INSPIRE is $63.0 million, $42.7 million (209.3%) more than the FY2012 estimated level of $20.4 million. All but $2.0 million of INSPIRE funding would come from R&RA.

[58] The FY2013 request for the I-Corps program is $19.0 million, $11.4 million (151.3%) more than the FY2012 estimated level of $7.5 million. All but $30,000 of this funding would come from R&RA accounts.

[59] NSF states that these funds would be used for grants to synthesize existing work, highlight trends and challenges, and (continued...)

---

initiative, Expeditions in Education (E^2). The goal for E^2 activities is to use current or emerging areas of science to address STEM education challenges. Funding would come from both R&RA and E&HR.[60] The request for E&HR also includes $121.5 million for the GRF program, $11.9 million (10.8%) over the FY2012 estimate. NSF seeks to reduce funding for the Integrative Graduate Education and Research Traineeship (IGERT) program by $8.1 million (-13.6%), from $59.8 million in FY2012 (estimated level) to $51.7 million in FY2013. Funding for minority-serving institutions (MSIs) would continue at FY2012 levels.[61] The FY2013 NSF budget request does not appear to include a specified funding source for Hispanic-serving institutions.

The President's FY2013 NSF budget request for MREFC is $196.2 million, $890,000 (-0.5%) below the FY2012 estimate of $197.1 million and $40.6 million (-17.2%) below the America COMPETES Reauthorization Act of 2010 (P.L. 111-358) authorized level of $236.8 million.[62] The request does not include funding for new MREFC projects in FY2013. As authorized by P.L. 112-55, NSF transferred $30.0 million from the R&RA account to MREFC in FY2012. This amount is reflected in the FY2013 request, which is $30.0 million more than the level Congress specified in FY2012. Two of MREFC's four funded projects in FY2013 are projected to be in the second-to-last year of their funding cycles.

Both the full House and the Senate Committee on Appropriations would fund E&HR and MREFC at close to requested levels in FY2013—$875.6 million and $196.2 million, respectively. Provisions in H.Rept. 112-463 express continued concern about contingency costs in the MREFC account. There are substantive differences between House and Senate appropriations committee recommendations for certain E&HR sub-accounts.[63] For example, H.Rept. 112-463 would provide the requested level of funding (e.g., no change from FY2012) for NSF's MSI programs, while S.Rept. 112-158 would provide a slight increase. H.Rept. 112-463 would fund the Advanced Technology Education (ATE) program at $69.0 million, while S.Rept. 112-158 would provide $64.0 million.[64] A third difference is between the two recommendations for NSF's Informal Science Education (ISE) program. H.Rept. 112-463 accepts the Administration's proposed changes to ISE, including a $13.6 million (-22.1%) reduction from the FY2012 estimate of $61.4 million. S.Rept. 112-158 rejects the requested reduction to ISE.[65]

The FY2013 request provides no increases for NSF's administrative accounts (e.g., Agency Operations and Award Management, National Science Board, and Inspector General) in FY2013. Both the full House and Senate Committee on Appropriations would provide the requested funding levels for these accounts in FY2013.

(...continued)

identify future needs.

[60] The total request for E^2 in FY2013 is $49.0 million, of which $20.5 million will come from E&HR.

[61] Funding sources for MSIs include the Historically-Black Colleges and Universities Undergraduate Program (HBCU-UP), Louis Stokes Alliances for Minority Participation (LSAMP), and the Tribal Colleges and Universities Program (TCUP), among others.

[62] As authorized by P.L. 112-55, NSF transferred $30.0 million from the R&RA account to MREFC in FY2012. This amount is reflected in the FY2013 request, which is $30.0 million more than the level Congress specified in FY2012.

[63] The FY2013 E&HR re-framing categorizes these accounts as Core R&D Programs.

[64] The FY2013 request for ATE is $64.0 million. The House Committee on Appropriations would off-set the recommended $5.0 million increase to ATE with an equivalent reduction to the E&HR contribution to the GRF.

[65] NSF also seeks to rename this program as "Advancing Informal STEM Learning" (AISL) in FY2013. Both appropriations committees accept this change.

Both the House and Senate appropriations committees express concerns about the "OneNSF Framework." As proposed, the OneNSF Framework seeks to enable operations across organizational and disciplinary boundaries. This NSF-wide initiative includes E^2, INSPIRE, and I-Corps; as well as other investments in smart systems, cyberinfrastructure, cybersecurity, and the Science, Engineering and Education for Sustainability (SEES) portfolio. NSF seeks increases over FY2012 estimated levels for six of the seven OneNSF Framework priorities. The Senate Committee on Appropriations recommends that NSF reduce funding for OneNSF activities and encourages the foundation to focus resources on core programs and infrastructure. The House Committee on Appropriations expresses concern about a perceived lack of administrative clarity in OneNSF activities and encourages NSF to promulgate clear standards and guidance on the administration of these activities.

Funding for other NSF-wide investments in the FY2013 request include the National Nanotechnology Initiative ($434.9 million), the Networking and Information Technology Research and Development program ($1.207 billion), and the U.S. Global Climate Change Research program ($332.9 million).

The FY2013 request also proposes cutting or consolidating 11 foundation programs, totaling $67.0 million. Most of these programs are in the research directorates and have reached their planned endpoints or are otherwise considered obsolete. As noted above, the House Committee on Appropriations rejects the proposed termination of the Communicating Science Broadly program.

Table 10. NSF Funding by Major Account

(budget authority in millions of dollars)

Account	FY2012 Estimate	FY2013 Authorized	FY2013 Request	H.R. 5326 House-passed	S. 2323 Senate Committee-reported
Biological Sciences	$712.4	n/s	$733.9	n/s	n/s
Computer and Information Science and Engineering	653.6	n/s	709.7	n/s	n/s
Engineering	826.2	n/s	876.3	n/s	n/s
Geosciences	885.3	n/s	906.4	n/s	n/s
Mathematical and Physical Sciences	1,309.0	n/s	1,345.2	n/s	n/s
Social, Behavioral, and Economic Sciences	254.3	n/s	259.6	n/s	n/s
Office of Cyberinfrastructure	211.6	n/s	218.3	n/s	n/s
Office of International Science and Engineering	49.9	n/s	51.3	n/s	n/s
U.S. Polar Programs	435.9	n/s	449.7	n/s	n/s
Integrative Activities	349.6	n/s	431.5	n/s	n/s
U.S. Arctic Research Commission	1.45	n/s	1.39	n/s	n/s

Account	FY2012 Estimate	FY2013 Authorized	FY2013 Request	H.R. 5326 House-passed	S. 2323 Senate Committee-reported
Research and Related Activities, Total	**$5,689.0**	**$6,638.0**	**$5,983.3**	**$5,942.7**	**$5,883.3**
Education and Human Resources	$829.0	$1,041.8	$875.6	$875.6	$875.6
Major Research Equipment and Facilities Construction	$197.1	$236.8	$196.2	$196.2	$196.2
Agency Operations and Award Management	$299.4	$363.7	$299.4	$299.4	$299.4
National Science Board	$4.4	$4.9	$4.4	$4.4	$4.4
Office of the Inspector General	$14.2	$15.0	$14.2	$14.2	$14.2
NSF, Total	**$7,033.1**	**$8,300.0**	**$7,373.1**	**$7,332.5**	**$7,273.1**

Source: Numbers in the "FY2012 Estimate" and "FY2013 Request" columns are from the FY2013 *NSF Budget Request to Congress*. Numbers in the "FY2013 Authorized" column are from the America COMPETES Reauthorization Act of 2010 (P.L. 111-358). Numbers in the "Full House" column are from H.Rept. 112-463 and H.R. 5326. Numbers in the "Senate Committee" column are from S.Rept. 112-158 and S. 2323.

Notes: "n/s" means "not specified." CRS was unable to identify a defined amount of funding for this account. Numbers are rounded.

National Aeronautics and Space Administration[66]

The Administration has requested $16.291 billion for NASA R&D in FY2013. This amount is 2.8% more than the $15.850 billion enacted for FY2012, but 11.3% below the $18.360 billion authorized by the NASA Authorization Act of 2010 (P.L. 111-267). The House bill would provide $16.049 billion. The Senate committee recommended $16.305 billion. For a breakdown of these amounts, see **Table 11**.

The requested increase in NASA R&D funding in FY2013, despite a requested decrease in funding for NASA as a whole, is made possible by the retirement of the space shuttles. The space shuttle program is classified as an operational expense, not R&D. The last shuttle flight was completed in July 2011, and the remaining closeout costs in FY2013 are expected to be only about $70 million compared with several billion dollars per year during shuttle operations.[67]

The Administration's $4.911 billion request for NASA's Science account in FY2013 is 3.5% less than the FY2012 appropriation. Funding for planetary science would decrease $308.1 million or 20.5%. Most of that proposed reduction is in the Mars exploration program, whose costs are reduced by the launch of the Mars Science Laboratory in November 2011, the planned launch of the Mars Atmosphere and Volatile Evolution Mission (MAVEN) in 2013, and the termination of NASA's participation (with the European Space Agency) in the 2016 and 2018 ExoMars

---

[66] This section was written by Daniel Morgan, Specialist in Science and Technology Policy, CRS Resources, Science, and Industry Division.

[67] The space shuttle program continued to receive an appropriation in FY2012, mostly to cover a shortfall in the defined benefit pension plan of the contractor that managed space shuttle operations.

missions. NASA is developing a new Mars exploration strategy that will integrate robotic missions funded by the Science account with human spaceflight and technology development activities in other accounts. Also in Science, funding for the James Webb Space Telescope (JWST) would increase $98.0 million or 18.5%. Following an independent review of JWST in October 2010, NASA developed a revised plan for the program in 2011. In the FY2012 appropriations conference report, Congress capped the formulation and development cost of JWST and mandated annual reports on the program by the Government Accountability Office. The House-passed bill would provide $5.095 billion for Science, or $184 million more than the request, including an increase of $88 million for a future Mars sample return mission. If NASA's new Mars strategy does not include a sample return mission, the $88 million would instead be devoted to a mission to Jupiter's moon Europa. The Senate committee recommended $5.021 billion for Science, or $110 million more than the request, including an increase of $100 million for Mars Exploration.

The request for Aeronautics is $551.5 million, a decrease of 3.2% from FY2012. Research on hypersonic entry, descent, and landing would be transferred to the Space Technology account, and most funding for air-breathing hypersonic flight systems would be eliminated. The hypersonic research remaining in the Aeronautics program would be combined with supersonic research to create a single project focusing on high-speed flight. The House-passed bill would provide $569.9 million. The Senate committee recommended the requested amount. Both committees expressed concern about the planned changes in NASA's hypersonics research. The House committee directed NASA to work with the Department of Defense to define agency roles and propose changes to the division of responsibilities. The Senate committee directed NASA to provide a report on how it plans to maintain hypersonics expertise either with its own funds or in collaboration with other agencies.

For Space Technology, the Administration has requested $699.0 million, an increase of 21.6% from FY2012. About half of the increase would be for technology demonstration missions designed to bridge the gap between early-stage development and operational use. In February 2012, the National Research Council (NRC) released its assessment of NASA's draft roadmaps for space technology development.[68] According to NASA, the Space Technology program is investing at some level in all 16 of the technology areas that the NRC report recommended for emphasis. The House-passed bill would provide $632.5 million for Space Technology. The Senate committee recommended $651.0 million and directed NASA to give priority to ongoing activities.

The Administration's request for Exploration in FY2013 is $3.933 billion, a 4.3% increase over FY2012 but 25.3% less than the authorized level. This account funds development of the Multipurpose Crew Vehicle (MPCV) and heavy-lift Space Launch System (SLS), which the 2010 authorization act mandated for human exploration of space beyond Earth orbit, as well as development of the commercial crew transportation systems that NASA intends to use for U.S. astronaut access to the International Space Station. The shortfall in Exploration funding relative to the authorization act may raise questions about the feasibility of NASA's planned human spaceflight program. NASA expects the first uncrewed flight of the SLS to occur in December 2017, and the first crewed flight in August 2021. If funding is appropriated at the requested level, NASA expects commercial crew transportation services to become available in early 2017; NASA officials state that a lower funding level will not permit this. The House-passed bill would

---

[68] National Research Council, *NASA Space Technology Roadmaps and Priorities: Restoring NASA's Technological Edge and Paving the Way for a New Era in Space*, download nap.edu/catalog.php?record_id=13354.

provide $3.712 billion for Exploration, including $112.5 million more than the request for the MPCV and SLS and their ground systems, and $329.7 million less than the request for commercial crew. The Senate committee recommended $3.909 billion. Within this total, the Senate committee provided $306.5 million more than the request for development of the MPCV and SLS and their associated ground systems, and $304.7 million less than the request for commercial crew.

The request for the International Space Station (ISS) is $3.008 billion, an increase of 6.3% from FY2012. Most of the proposed increase would be for ISS crew and cargo transportation provided by international partners and commercial companies. (The first commercial cargo flight to the ISS took place in May 2012.) The House-passed bill would provide $2.990 billion for the ISS. The Senate committee recommended $2.958 billion.

The Senate committee recommended $1.641 billion for NASA to acquire operational satellites for NOAA. In the past, this work has been carried out by NASA on a cost-reimbursement basis using funds appropriated to NOAA. Because the programs covered by the proposal are considered acquisitions, not R&D, transferring the appropriation from NOAA to NASA would not directly affect NASA R&D funding.

Table 11. NASA R&D

(in millions of dollars)

	FY2011 Actual[a]	FY2012 Enacted	FY2013 Authorized	FY2013 Request	H.R. 5326 House-passed	S. 2323 Senate Committee-reported
Science	$4,919.7	$5,090.0	$5,509.6	$4,911.2	$5,095.0	$5,021.1
Earth Science	1,721.9	1,765.7	2,089.5	1,784.8	1,775.0	1,784.7
Planetary Science	1,450.8	1,500.4	1,591.2	1,192.3	1,400.0	1,292.3
Astrophysics	631.1	672.0	1,149.1[b]	659.4	650.0	669.4
James Webb Space Telescope	476.8	529.6	0.0[b]	627.6	628.0	627.6
Heliophysics	639.2	622.3	679.8	647.0	642.0	647.0
Aeronautics	533.5	569.9	590.0	551.5	569.9	551.5
Space Technology	456.3	575.0	515.0	699.0	632.5	651.0
Exploration	3,821.2	3,770.8	5,264.0	3,932.8	3,711.9	3,908.9
Exploration Systems Development	2,982.1	3,060.0	4,040.0	2,769.4	2,881.9	3,075.9
Commercial Spaceflight	606.8	406.0	500.0	829.7	500.0	525.0
Exploration R&D	232.3	304.8	724.0	333.7	330.0	308.0
International Space Station	2,713.6	2,830.0	3,129.4	3,007.6	2,990.0	2,957.6
Subtotal R&D	**12,444.3**	**12,835.7**	**15,008.0**	**13,102.1**	**12,999.3**	**13,090.1**
Non-R&D Programs[c]	2,614.4	1,579.3	1,308.3	1,142.6	1,133.0	2,808.0
Cross-Agency Support[d]	2,956.4	2,995.0	3,276.8	2,847.5	2,717.5	2,822.5
Associated with R&D	2,443.1	2,666.9	3,014.1	2,619.1	2,499.6	2,591.5
Construction & Environ. C&R[d]	432.9	390.0	366.9	619.2	598.0	679.0
Associated with R&D	357.7	347.3	337.5	569.5	550.1	623.4

	FY2011 Actuala	FY2012 Enacted	FY2013 Authorized	FY2013 Request	H.R. 5326 House-passed	S. 2323 Senate Committee-reported
Total R&D	15,245.2	15,849.8	18,359.5	16,290.7	16,049.0	16,305.0
Total NASA	18,448.0	17,800.0e	19,960.0	17,711.4	17,447.8	19,399.6

Source: FY2011 actual and FY2013 request from NASA's FY2013 congressional budget justification, http://www.nasa.gov/news/budget/. FY2012 enacted from P.L. 112-55 and H.Rept. 112-284. FY2013 authorized from NASA Authorization Act of 2010 (P.L. 111-267), Sec. 103. FY2013 House from H.R. 5326 as passed by the House and H.Rept. 112-463. FY2013 Senate Committee from S. 2323 as reported and S.Rept. 112-158.

Notes:

a. Includes rescissions.

b. James Webb Space Telescope was included in Astrophysics in the authorization act.

c. Space Shuttle, Space and Flight Support, Education, Inspector General, and NOAA Operational Satellite Acquisition. (The last of these is only present in the FY2013 Senate Committee bill.)

d. Allocation between R&D and non-R&D is estimated by CRS in proportion to the underlying program amounts (omitting NOAA Operational Satellite Acquisition, for comparability) in order to allow calculation of a total for R&D. The Cross-Agency Support and Construction and Environmental Compliance and Remediation accounts consist mostly of indirect costs for other programs, assessed in proportion to their direct costs.

e. Does not reflect a rescission of $30 million in unobligated funds from prior years.

Department of Commerce

National Institute of Standards and Technology[69]

The National Institute of Standards and Technology (NIST) is a laboratory of the Department of Commerce with a mandate to increase the competitiveness of U.S. companies through appropriate support for industrial development of precompetitive, generic technologies and the diffusion of government-developed technological advances to users in all segments of the American economy. NIST research also provides the measurement, calibration, and quality assurance techniques that underpin U.S. commerce, technological progress, improved product reliability, manufacturing processes, and public safety.

The President's FY2013 budget requests $857.0 million for NIST, an increase of 14.1% over the $750.8 million appropriated in FY2012. Included in this figure is $648.0 million for research and development in the Scientific and Technical Research and Services (STRS) account, 14.3% above the FY2012 amount of $567.0 million. Under the Industrial Technology Services (ITS) account, the Manufacturing Extension Partnership (MEP) program is to receive $128.0 million, a 0.3% decrease from FY2012 funding of $128.4 million. Also included in ITS, the Administration again proposes the creation of a new activity, the Advanced Manufacturing Technology Consortia (AMTech), which was not funded when it was included in the FY2012 budget. In FY2013,

[69] This section was written by Wendy H. Schacht, Specialist in Science and Technology Policy, CRS Resources, Science, and Industry Division.

support for AMTech would total $21.0 million. The requested appropriation for the construction budget is $60.0 million, 8.3% above the $55.4 million for FY2012.

In addition to the appropriations included in the budget request that are to be addressed through the annual appropriations process, the Administration proposes two new programs that are to be funded through mandatory appropriations.[70] Up to $300.0 million generated by the proceeds of the spectrum auction is to support the Wireless Innovation Fund and $1.000 billion is to be provided for establishment of the National Network for Manufacturing Innovation.

S. 2323, as reported from the Senate Committee on Appropriations, would provide $826.0 million in FY2013 funding for NIST, 10.0% above the FY2012 appropriation but 3.6% below the Administration's request. Support for the STRS account totals $623.0 million, 9.9% more than the previous fiscal year and 3.9% less than the President proposes. MEP would receive $128.5 million, 0.1% above the FY2012 figure and 0.4% more than the budget request, while AMTech would be financed at $14.5 million, 31.0% below what the Administration included in the budget proposal. The $60.0 million in the construction account is 8.3% more than in FY2012 and the same as the budget request.

The bill reported from the House Committee on Appropriations, H.R. 5326, funds NIST at $830.2 million, an increase of 10.6% over FY2012, 3.1% less than the Administration's budget, and 0.5% more than the Senate figure. The $621.2 million for the STRS account is an increase of 9.6% above the earlier fiscal year, but 4.1% less than the President's request, and 0.3% less than the amount included in S. 2323. Financing for MEP would total $128.0 million, 0.3% less than FY2012, the same as the budget proposal, and 0.4% below the Senate-reported bill. AMTech would receive $21.0 million, equal to the amount in the Administration request, and 44.8% more than in S. 2323. The $60.0 million included for construction is the same as that in the proposed budget and the Senate bill.

NIST's extramural programs (currently the Manufacturing Extension Partnership),which are directed toward increased private sector commercialization, have been a source of contention. Some Members of Congress have expressed skepticism over a "technology policy" based on providing federal funds to industry for the development of "pre-competitive generic" technologies. This approach, coupled with pressures to balance the federal budget, has led to proposals for the elimination of these activities. In 2007, the Advanced Technology Program was terminated and replaced by the Technology Innovation Program which operated until support was withdrawn in the final FY2012 appropriation. An additional extramural program, AMTech, introduced in the FY2012 budget request, also was not funded.[71]

Increases in spending for NIST laboratories that perform the research essential to the mission responsibilities of the agency have tended to remain small. As part of the American Competitiveness Initiative, announced by former President Bush in the 2006 State of the Union address, the Administration stated its intention to double funding over 10 years for "innovation-

---

[70] Mandatory spending is typically provided in permanent or multi-year appropriations contained in the authorizing law, and therefore, the funding becomes available automatically each year, without legislative action by Congress. For additional information on mandatory spending, see CRS Report RL33074, *Mandatory Spending Since 1962*, by D. Andrew Austin and Mindy R. Levit, Mandatory Spending Sine 1962, by D. Andrew Austin and Mindy R. Levit.

[71] For additional information on the MEP and TIP programs, see CRS Report RS22815, *The Technology Innovation Program*, and CRS Report 97-104, *Manufacturing Extension Partnership Program: An Overview*, both by Wendy H. Schacht.

enabling research" done, in part, at NIST through its "core" programs (defined as the STRS account and the construction budget). In April 2009, President Obama indicated his decision to double the budget of key science agencies, including NIST, over the next 10 years. In President Obama's FY2011 budget the timeframe for doubling slipped to 11 years; his FY2012 budget was intentionally silent on a timeframe for doubling. While the final FY2012 appropriation did not include an increase in support for NIST, there was a 14.0% increase in funding for R&D under the STRS account.[72] The Administration's FY2013 budget proposal would increase support for NIST 14.1% (excluding mandatory appropriations) and includes a 14.3% increase in the STRS account. S. 2323 contains a 10.0% increase in funding for NIST and a 9.9% increase in funding for the STRS account, while H.R. 5326 includes a 10.6% increase for NIST and a 9.6% increase for STRS.

Table 12. NIST

(in millions of dollars)

NIST Program	FY2011 Enacted[a]	FY2012 Enacted P.L. 112-55	FY2013 Request	H.R. 5326 House-passed	S. 2323 Senate Committee-reported
Scientific and Technical Research and Services[b]	497.4	567.0	648.0	621.2	623.0
Industrial Technology Services					
Technology Innovation Program	44.8	0	0	0	0
Manufacturing Extension Partnership	128.4	128.4	128.0	128.0	128.5
Baldrige Program	9.6	0	0	0	0
AMTech		0	21.0	21.0	14.5
Construction	69.9	55.4	60.0	60.0	60.0
NIST Total[c]	**750.1**	**750.8**	**857.0**	**830.2**	**826.0**
Mandatory Appropriations					
Wireless Innovation Fund			300.0[d]		
National Network for Manufacturing Innovation			1,000.0		

Sources: NIST website (available at http://www.nist.gov/public_affairs/budget.htm), P.L. 111-117, P.L. 112-10, and Administration's FY2012 Budget Request.

Notes:

a. Includes a 0.2% across the board rescission.

b. Excludes FY2011 funding for the Baldrige National Quality Program; funding for this program is included in FY2011 Enacted columns under ITS for comparison purposes.

c. Totals may differ from the sum of the components due to rounding.

d. Funds are to be generated by spectrum auction.

---

[72] For additional information on NIST, see CRS Report 95-30, *The National Institute of Standards and Technology: An Appropriations Overview*.

National Oceanic and Atmospheric Administration[73]

The Commerce Department's National Oceanic and Atmospheric Administration (NOAA) conducts scientific research in areas such as ecosystems, climate, global climate change, weather, and oceans; supplies information on the oceans and atmosphere; and manages coastal and marine organisms and environments. NOAA was created in 1970 by Reorganization Plan No. 4.[74] The reorganization was intended to unify elements of the nation's environmental activities and to provide a systematic approach for monitoring, analyzing, and protecting the environment.

NOAA's R&D efforts focus on three areas: climate; weather and air quality; and ocean, coastal, and Great Lakes resources. Furthermore, NOAA's R&D efforts support the four long-term goals of NOAA's Next Generation Strategic Plan. The goals include (1) climate adaptation and mitigation, (2) weather-ready nation,[75] (3) healthy oceans, and (4) resilient coastal communities and economies.[76]

For FY2013, President Obama requests $650.6 million in R&D funding for NOAA, a 12.9% increase in funding from the FY2012 level of $580.6 million. R&D accounts for 12.9% of NOAA's total FY2013 discretionary budget request of $5.055 billion. The R&D request consists of $452 million for research (69.4%), $56 million for development (8.6%), and $143 million for R&D equipment (22.0%). Excluding equipment, about $371 million (73.0%) of the R&D request would fund intramural programs and $137 million (27.0%) would fund extramural programs.[77]

NOAA's administrative structure has five line offices that reflect its diverse mission: National Ocean Service (NOS); National Marine Fisheries Service (NMFS); National Environmental Satellite, Data, and Information Service (NESDIS); National Weather Service (NWS); and Office of Oceanic and Atmospheric Research (OAR). In addition to NOAA's five line offices, Program Support (PS), a cross-cutting budget activity, includes the Office of Marine and Aviation Operations (OMAO).

Table 13 provides R&D funding levels by line office for FY2011, FY2012, and the FY2013 request.[78] On April 19, 2012, the Senate Committee on Appropriations reported S. 2323, and on May 10, 2012, the House passed H.R. 5326. Neither of the appropriations bills or accompanying committee reports specify R&D funding levels for NOAA, but total recommended agency funding has been provided in **Table 13** for context.

---

[73] This section was written by Harold F. Upton, Analyst in Natural Resources Policy, CRS Resources, Science, and Industry Division.

[74] "Reorganization Plan No. 4 of 1970," 35 *Fed. Reg.* 15627-15630, October 6, 1970; also, see http://www.lib noaa.gov/noaainfo/heritage/ReorganizationPlan4.html.

[75] According to NOAA a weather-ready nation is envisioned as a society that is prepared for and responds to weather-related events.

[76] National Oceanic and Atmospheric Administration, *National Oceanic and Atmospheric Administration FY 2012 Budget Summary*, National Oceanic and Atmospheric Administration, Washington, DC, February 2011, http://www.corporateservices noaa.gov/nbo/fy12_bluebook/chapter7_Research_Development.pdf.

[77] National Oceanic and Atmospheric Administration, *National Oceanic and Atmospheric Administration FY 2013 Budget Summary*, National Oceanic and Atmospheric Administration, Washington, DC, March 2012, http://www.corporateservices noaa.gov/nbo/13bluebook_highlights html.

[78] Stacy Dennery, Budget Analyst, NOAA Budget Office, e-mail, March 7, 2012.

Table 13. NOAA R&D

(in millions of dollars)

Line Offices	FY2011 Enacted[a]	FY2012 Enacted	FY2013 Request	H.R. 5326 House-passed	S. 2323 Senate Committee-reported[b]
National Ocean Service	$71.6	64.5	80.0		
National Marine Fisheries Service	55.4	52.0	59.7		
Office of Oceanic and Atmospheric Research	390.0	348.1	378.9		
National Weather Service	21.5	20.4	21.6		
National Environmental Satellite, Data, and Information Service	28.9	26.8	35.5		
Office of Marine and Aviation Operations[c]	61.8	68.8	74.9		
Total R&D[d]	**629.0**	**580.6**	**650.6**		
NOAA Total	**4,588.0**	**4,893.7**	**5,054.5**	**4,944.7**	**3,418.7**

Sources: Stacy Dennery, NOAA Budget Office, e-mail, March 7, 2012.

Notes:

a. Includes rescissions.

b. The large difference in the NOAA total is due to the recommended transfer of satellite acquisition to NASA.

c. All OMAO R&D funding is for equipment.

d. Totals may differ from the sum of the components due to rounding.

Department of Agriculture[79]

U.S. Department of Agriculture (USDA) research and education activities are included in four organizations: Agricultural Research Service (ARS), National Institute of Food and Agriculture (NIFA),[80] Economic Research Service (ERS), and National Agricultural Statistics Service (NASS). The Administration's FY2013 for research and education activities in USDA is $2.656 billion, a decrease of 2.2% from the FY2012 enacted level of $2.715 billion. (See **Table 14**.) Even with the proposed decline in funding in the FY2013 request, Secretary of Agriculture Tom Vilsack stated that

> To help sustain record farm income, we will invest in research and development to improve agricultural productivity. The budget has made a 23% increase in funding for our premier competitive grants program to support the most worthy projects and continues support for in-

---

[79] This section was written by Christine M. Matthews, Specialist in Science and Technology Policy, CRS Resources, Science, and Industry Division.

[80] NIFA was formerly the Cooperative State Research, Education, and Extension Service (CSREES).

house research and the land grant universities. We'll continue our efforts to combat destructive pests and disease that threaten crops and livestock.[81]

The Agricultural Research Service is USDA's in-house basic and applied research agency, and operates approximately 100 laboratories nationwide. The ARS also includes the National Agricultural Library, a primary information resource on food, agriculture, and natural resource sciences. The ARS laboratories focus on efficient food and fiber production, development of new products and uses for agricultural commodities, development of effective biocontrols for pest management, and support of USDA regulatory and technical assistance programs. The President requested $1.130 billion for ARS in FY2013, $4.0 million above the FY2012 enacted level. The FY2013 request proposes $50.4 million in program reallocations to address the nation's most critical research needs, including a reallocation of $4.0 million for research to develop integrated, sustainable production systems that will improve food production efficiency and protect the environment, and a reallocation of $3.2 million for an integrated research initiative for floral and nursery crops, collectively the third largest crop in the nation.

There is also the proposed elimination of lower priority extramural projects. Funding from proposed discontinued ARS projects will be redirected to agency research priorities. Priorities in the FY2013 request include the conversion of agricultural products into biobased products and biofuels; development of new measures to control bovine tuberculosis and bovine respiratory diseases; domestic and global market opportunities; new varieties and hybrids of feedstocks; and new healthier foods with decreased caloric density. ARS proposes to expand its research on detection methods and countermeasures to foreign animal diseases that could result in catastrophic losses. The FY2013 request proposes an increase of approximately $25.0 million for research directed at improving American agriculture's adaptability to environmental challenges. This proposal is a result of the recommendations contained in a 2011 report of the President's Council of Advisors on Science and Technology stating the need for improved accounting of ecosytem services and increased protection of the environment.

The National Institute of Food and Agriculture was established in Title VII, Section 7511 of the Food, Conservation, and Energy Act of 2008 (P.L. 110-246, also known as the 2008 farm bill). In the FY2013 budget request, NIFA is to support larger and longer-term research efforts on issues related to the viability of agriculture. NIFA is responsible for developing partnerships between the federal and state components of agricultural research, extension, and institutions of higher education. NIFA distributes funds to State Agricultural Experiment Stations, State Cooperative Extension Systems, land-grant universities, and other institutions and organizations that conduct agricultural research, education, and outreach. Included in these partnerships is funding for research at 1862 land-grant institutions, 1890 historically black colleges and universities, 1994 tribal land-grant colleges, and Hispanic-serving institutions.[82] Funding is distributed to the states through competitive awards, statutory formula funding, and special grants. The FY2013 request provides $1.271 billion for NIFA, $82.6 million below the FY2012 enacted level.

The Administration's FY2013 request for NIFA emphasizes competitive, peer-reviewed allocation of research funding to generate solutions for the most critical needs of agriculture. Funding for

---

[81] U.S. Department of Agriculture, "Remarks as Prepared for Delivery:Agriculture Secretary Vilsack Before the House Subcommittee on Agriculture, Rural Development, Food and Drug Administration, and Related Agencies," February 17, 2012, http://www.usda.gov/wps/portal/usda/!ut/p/c5/04_SB8K8xLLM9MsszPy8xBz9CPos_gA.

[82] The numbers 1862, 1890, and 1994 in this context refer to the years laws were enacted creating these classifications of colleges and universities.

FY2013 includes support for grant management, as well as for programs that are responsive to critical national issues such as agricultural security, local and regional emergencies, zoonotic diseases, climate change, childhood obesity, and pest risk management. The request also provides funding for programs that support minority-serving institutions and their recipients.

In the past three years, five virtual Regional Research Centers have been established focused on developing new feedstocks and more efficient ways to produce biofuel. In addition, five new biorefineries have been established. In the FY2013 request, funding is provided to support 235 advanced biofuel producers. USDA has identified approximately 50,000 acres in nine project areas to support the production of new feedstocks, nonfeedstocks, wind energy projects, and anaerobic digesters.

NIFA is responsible for administering the agency's primary competitive research grants program, the Agriculture and Food Research Initiative (AFRI). In addition to supporting fundamental and applied science in agriculture, USDA maintains that the AFRI makes a significant contribution to developing the next generation of agricultural scientists by providing graduate students with opportunities to work on research projects. A focus of these efforts is to provide increased opportunities for minority and under-served communities in agricultural science. The FY2013 request provides $325.0 million for the AFRI, a proposed increase of $61.0 million over the FY2012 enacted level. Major initiatives of the AFRI include proposed funding of $30.0 million for alternative and renewable energy research to develop high-quality, cost-effective feedstocks for biofuel production; $3.7 million for research to address the adaptation of production systems to climate varieties; $7.2 million for international food security to improve research and extension efforts on sustainable plant and animal production systems; and $3.2 million for AFRI's Foundational Research Program. Additional research is to be directed toward global climate change research to develop mitigation capabilities for agricultural production, and support for an integrated food safety research program with the potential for improving the understanding of disease-causing microorganisms. The request also supports research in agricultural genomics, emerging issues in food and agricultural security, the ecology and economics of biological invasions, and plant biotechnology. In addition, it is anticipated that water research will extend beyond water quality to include water availability, reuse, and conservation.

The FY2013 budget request proposes $77.4 million for ERS, slightly below the FY2012 enacted level of $77.7 million. The request includes the termination of low-priority programs. The ERS supports economic and social science information analysis on agriculture, rural development, food, commodity markets, and the environment. ERS collects and disseminates data concerning USDA programs and policies to various stakeholders.

Funding for the National Agricultural Statistics Service is proposed at $179.5 million in the FY2013 request, $20.9 million above the FY2012 enacted level. The FY2013 request includes support for improving research efforts in analyzing the impacts of bioenergy production, and for examining concerns pertaining to feedstock storage, transportation networks, and commodity production. Other research areas receiving support include production and use of biomass materials; stocks and prices of distillers' grains; current and proposed ethanol production plants; the chemical use data series on major row crops; post harvest chemical use; and alternating annual fruit, nuts, and vegetable chemical use. Funding is to increase $20.9 million in support the 2012 Census of Agriculture, an anticipated increase related to the cyclical nature of the five-year census program.

On April 26, 2012, the Senate Committee on Appropriations reported S. 2375, Agriculture, Rural Development, Food and Drug Administration and Related Agencies Appropriation Act, FY2013 (S.Rept. 112-163). The ARS is proposed at $1,101.9 million, slightly below the FY2013 request of $1,102.6 million and $7.3 million above the FY2012 estimate of $1,094.6 million. Conferees stated that they are not in agreement with the Administration regarding the closing of six research laboratories and the termination of extramural research. In addition, conferees recommended funding for the repair and maintenance of the National Agricultural Library. Included in the report is a directive for the USDA to submit a capital asset plan by July 1, 2012, for maintaining and constructing facilities to meet ARS' research priorities. Conferees stated that the agency did not adequately budget for the closure of six research laboratories. They further indicated that the closure of facilities can be costly and does not always translate into immediate, real savings. Language in the report directs the USDA to " specifically identify costs associated with closing a location and relocating employees."[83]

Research and education activities are proposed at $738.6 million in S. 2375, $5.9 million above the Administration's request and approximately $33.0 million above the FY2012 level. The bill proposes $77.4 million for the ERS, level with FY2013 and a slight increase above the FY2012 appropriation. The FY2013 includes continued funding for the Organic Production and Market Data Initiative. Funding for the NASS is proposed at $179.5 million in S. 2375, level with the Administration's request and $20.9 million above the FY2012 estimated level.

Table 14. U.S. Department of Agriculture R&D

(in millions of dollars)

	FY2011 Actual	FY2012 Enacted	FY2013 Request
Agricultural Research Service			
Product Quality/Value Added	105.0	101.0	93.2
Livestock Production	81.0	76.0	71.0
Crop Production	232.0	229.0	229.0
Food Safety	107.0	106.0	108.0
Livestock Protection	79.0	76.3	78.0
Crop Protection	203.0	194.0	184.0
Human Nutrition	85.0	85.1	84.0
Environmental Stewardship	201.0	189.0	214.1
National Agricultural Library	21.0	21.0	21.0
Repair and Maintenance of Facilities	17.0	17.2	20.3
Subtotal	**1,131.0**	**1,094.6**	**1,102.6**
Trust Funds	31.0	31.0	27.0
Total, ARS	**1,162.0**	**1,125.6**	**1,129.6**

---

[83] Senate Committee on Appropriations, *Agriculture, Rural Development, Food and Drug Administration, and Related Agencies Appropriations Bill, 2013*, S.Rept. 112-163, Report to accompany S. 2375, 112th Cong., 2nd Sess., April 26, 2012, p. 21.

	FY2011 Actual	FY2012 Enacted	FY2013 Request
National Institute of Food and Agriculture[a]			
Hatch Act Formula	236.0	236.0	235.0
Cooperative Forestry Research	33.0	33.0	33.0
Earmarked Projects and Grants	2.8	0.0	1.2
Agriculture & Food Research Initiative	264.0	264.0	325.0
Federal Administration	15.0	13.0	15.0
Higher Education Programs[b]	48.0	46.8	47.8
Other Programs	100.2	112.8	75.7
Subtotal, Research and Education Activities	***699.0***	***705.6***	***732.7***
Extension Activities			
Smith-Lever Sections 3b&c	294.0	294.0	292.0
Extension Activities at 1994 Institutions	4.0	4.0	4.0
1890 Colleges, Tuskegee, & West Virginia State University Colleges	93.0	93.0	93.0
Other Extension Programs	88.0	84.2	73.5
Subtotal, Extension Activities	***479.0***	***475.2***	***462.5***
Integrated Activities	37.0	21.5	43.5
Mandatory and Farm Bill Programs	141.0	151.0	32.0
Total, NIFA[c]	**1,356.0**	**1,353.3**	**1,270.7**
Economic Research Service	**81.8**	**77.7**	**77.4**
National Agricultural Statistics Service	**156.4**	**158.6**	**179.5**
Total, Research, Education, and Economics	**2,756.2**	**2,715.2**	**2,657.2**

Sources: U.S. Department of Agriculture, *FY2013 Budget Summary and Annual Performance Plan,* February 2012.

Note: Totals and subtotals may differ from the sum of the components due to rounding.

a. Funding levels are contained in the U.S. Department of Agriculture FY2013 Budget Summary and Annual Performance Plan, February 2012. Formerly CSREES. NIFA was established in Title VII of the 2008 Farm Bill.

b. Higher Education includes capacity building grants, Hispanic-Serving Institution Education Grants Program, Two-Year Postsecondary, and Agriculture in the K-12 Classroom, Higher Education Challenge Grants, Improve the Quality of Life in Rural America, and others.

c. Program totals may or may not include set-asides (non-add) or contingencies.

Department of the Interior[84]

The Administration has requested $910.8 million in R&D funding for the Department of the Interior (DOI) for FY2013, $64.0 million (7.6%) above its FY2012 funding level of $846.8 million. (See **Table 15**.) The U.S. Geological Survey (USGS) accounts for most of DOI's R&D

---

[84] This section was written by John F. Sargent, Specialist in Science and Technology Policy, CRS Resources, Science, and Industry Division.

($726.5 million, 79.8% of total DOI R&D). USGS is also the most R&D-intensive agency in DOI, with approximately two-thirds of its FY2011 appropriations devoted to R&D activities.

Funding for DOI R&D is generally included in line items that also include non-R&D funding. Therefore it is not possible to know precisely how much of the funding provided for in appropriations bills will be allocated to R&D unless funding is provided for at the full level of the request. In general, R&D funding levels are determined only after DOI agencies report on their allocation of appropriations. In February 2012, DOI provided detailed information to CRS on R&D funding levels proposed by the President for each of its agencies and for broad program areas; this data was used for the analysis in this section.[85]

U.S. Geological Survey

All USGS funding is provided through a single account, Surveys, Investigations, and Research (SIR). USGS R&D is conducted under seven activity/program areas that constitute DOI's Surveys, Investigations, and Research (SIR) portfolio: Ecosystems; Climate and Land Use Change; Energy, Minerals, and Environmental Health; Natural Hazards; Water Resources, Core Science Systems; and Administration and Enterprise Information.

The President's FY2013 budget request for USGS includes $726.5 million for R&D, an increase of $51.0 million (7.6%) over the FY2012 R&D funding level of $675.5 million. Among the largest R&D increases in the USGS portfolio are for Science Synthesis, Analysis, and Research which would increase by $11.3 million (74.9%) and Climate Change Science Support for DOI Bureaus which would increase $6.6 million (273.9%).

In the DOI budget classification Natural Hazards, the President's budget would increase funding for Earthquake Hazards by $5.4 million (15.1%) and for Coastal and Marine Geology by $5.4 million (12.3%). Within Ecosystems, three areas receive specific attention: Fisheries—Aquatic & Endangered Resources, up $4.5 million (20.1%); Terrestrial, Freshwater, and Marine Environments, up $5.8 million (15.9%); and Invasive Species, up $4.6 million (35.5%). Within Energy, Minerals, and Environmental Health, the President's budget includes an increase of $3.2 million (11.7%) for Energy Resources and a reduction of $4.0 million (-8.0%) for Mineral Resources.

The President sought to eliminate Water Resources Research Act (WRRA) program funding in FY2012, but Congress opted to provide $6.5 million for the program. WRRA provides funding to 54 Water Resources Research Institutes at land grant universities—one in each state, the District of Columbia, Puerto Rico, the U.S. Virgin Islands, and Guam for the federal-state partnership in water resources research, education, and information transfer. In his FY2013 budget, the President again seeks to eliminate funding (-$6.5 million) for the WRRA program According to the President's budget, "The elimination of this program allows the USGS to redirect scarce funds to other priority issues, such as WaterSMART."[86] The WaterSMART program is a multidisciplinary USGS effort focused on improving understanding of the linkages between water quantity, quality, and the environment. In FY2012, approximately $8.0 million was directed to

---

[85] Private email correspondence between the DOI budget office and CRS, February 17, 2012.

[86] Department of the Interior, *Budget Justifications and Performance Information, FY2013: U.S. Geological Survey*, p. B-41, http://www.doi.gov/budget/2013/data/greenbook/FY2013_USGS_Greenbook.pdf.

WaterSMART activities (R&D and non-R&D); the President's FY2013 budget includes funding of $21.0 million for WaterSMART activities, an increase of $13.0 million (163.0%).

Other DOI Agencies

Under the President's FY2013 budget, the Fish and Wildlife Service would receive $55.3 million, an increase of $6.8 million (14.0%) over its FY2012 level, the second largest R&D increase among the DOI agencies. The Bureau of Land Management would receive $18.6 million, an increase of $2.0 million (12.0%). The Bureau of Reclamation would receive $13.0 million, up $1.0 million (8.3%). The National Park Service would receive $31.5 million, an increase of $0.5 million (1.7%). The Bureau of Ocean Energy Management (BOEM) would receive $39.1 million in FY2013 under the President's budget, an increase of $0.5 million (1.3%) over FY2012. The Bureau of Safety and Environmental Enforcement (BSEE) would receive $26.9 million, $2.1 million (8.7%) more than in FY2012.

Table 15. Department of the Interior R&D

(in millions of dollars)

	FY2011 Actual	FY2012 Enacted	FY2013 Request
U.S. Geological Survey	640.0	675.5	726.5
Bureau of Land Management	16.6	16.6	18.6
Bureau of Reclamation	14.1	12.0	13.0
National Park Service	26.3	30.9	31.5
Fish and Wildlife Service	47.0	48.5	55.3
Bureau of Ocean Energy Management, Regulation, and Enforcement[a]	35.6	—	—
Bureau of Ocean Energy Management[a]	—	38.6	39.1
Bureau of Safety and Environmental Enforcement[a]	—	24.7	26.9
Total, DOI R&D[b]	**779.6**	**846.8**	**910.8**

Source: Unpublished data provided to CRS by the Department of the Interior.

Notes:

a.   On October 1, 2011, the Bureau of Ocean Energy Management, Regulation and Enforcement (BOEMRE), formerly the Minerals Management Service (MMS), was replaced by the Bureau of Ocean Energy Management and the Bureau of Safety and Environmental Enforcement as part of a major reorganization.

b.   Totals may differ from the sum of the components due to rounding.

Environmental Protection Agency[87]

The U.S. Environmental Protection Agency (EPA), the regulatory agency responsible for carrying out a number of environmental pollution control laws, funds a broad portfolio of research and development (R&D) activities to provide scientific tools and knowledge to support decisions relating to preventing, regulating, and abating environmental pollution. Beginning in FY2006, EPA has been funded through the Interior, Environment, and Related Agencies appropriations bill. Most of EPA's scientific research activities are funded within the agency's Science and Technology (S&T) appropriations account. This account is funded by a "base" appropriation and a transfer from the Hazardous Substance Superfund (Superfund) account. These transferred funds are dedicated to research on more effective methods to clean up contaminated sites.

The President's FY2013 budget request of $830.5 million for the EPA S&T account, including transfers from the Superfund account, is $13.8 million (1.7%) above the $816.7 million included for FY2012 in the Consolidated Appropriations Act, 2012 (P.L. 112-74 Title II of Division E, H.R. 2055) enacted December 23, 2011. The amount included in the FY2013 budget request for the EPA's S&T account (including transfers) represents roughly 10% of the agency's total $8.34 billion request for FY2013. (FY2012 enacted amounts presented in this section of the report reflect the application of 0.16% rescission.[88])

As indicated in **Table 16** below, the total base requested funding for the S&T account is an increase above the FY2012 enacted level, but below the FY2011 enacted amount for this account. The $23.2 million proposed transfer from the Superfund account for FY2013 is roughly the same as the $23.0 million transferred in FY2012, but $3.6 million less than the $26.8 million transferred in FY2012. As indicated in EPA's FY2013 Congressional budget justification[89] and reflected in the table, the requested base amount for the S&T account includes both increases and decreases of varying levels for the individual EPA research program and activity line-items identified within the account when compared with the enacted FY2012 appropriations. For some activities, the amount of the request for FY2013 remained relatively flat compared to the prior year appropriation. The FY2013 request also reflects the reorganization of the EPA S&T budget presentation of certain program activities below the appropriations account level accepted by the Conferees for FY2012,[90] including consolidation and modifications of specific line-items. The reorganization makes it difficult to make direct comparisons with the FY2011 enacted levels for sub-account level line items as reflected in **Table 16** below. Program areas revised as part of the

---

[87] This section was written by Robert Esworthy, Specialist in Environmental Policy, CRS Resources, Science, and Industry Division. For a broader overview of EPA's FY2013 appropriations, see CRS Report R42520, *Environmental Protection Agency (EPA): Appropriations for FY2013*, by Robert Esworthy et al.; for FY2012 see CRS Report R41896, *Interior, Environment, and Related Agencies: FY2012 Appropriations*, coordinated by Carol Hardy Vincent, and CRS Report R42332, *Environmental Protection Agency (EPA) FY2012 Appropriations*, by Robert Esworthy.

[88] Title IV, Division E of P.L. 112-74, Section 436(a): "Across-the-board Rescissions—There is hereby rescinded an amount equal to 0.16 percent of the budget authority provided for fiscal year 2012 for any discretionary appropriation in titles I through IV of this Act." FY2012 enacted amounts presented in EPA's FY2013 Congressional Budget Justification include the subsequent application of the rescission. The total FY2012 enacted appropriations for the EPA S&T account, including transfers, in P.L. 112-74 was $818.0 million prior to the rescission.

[89] U.S. EPA, *Fiscal year FY2013 Justification of Appropriation Estimates for the Committee on Appropriations: Science and Technology*, http://www.epa.gov/planandbudget/FY_2012_CJ_VV_rev.pdf, PDF pp. 74-200.

[90] Reorganized as proposed by the President for FY2012, U.S. EPA, *Fiscal Year FY2012 Justification of Appropriation Estimates for the Committee on Appropriations: Science and Technology*, http://www.epa.gov/planandbudget/annualplan/fy2013.html#FY13budget, PDF pp. 74-248.

---

modifications within the S&T account include Clean Air and Climate; Research: Air, Climate and Energy; Research: Chemical Safety and Sustainability; and Research: Sustainability and Healthy Communities.

Examples of FY2013 requested reductions below the FY2012 levels for programmatic areas within EPA's S&T appropriations account, include $165.7 million for Sustainable and Healthy Communities (human health and ecosystem) Research, $5.0 million (nearly 3.0%) less than FY2012 enacted; and $40.1 million for EPA's Homeland Security research activities,[91] $1.9 million (4.5 %) less than FY2011. The largest requested decrease for FY2013 below FY2012 enacted levels within the S&T account was for the Climate Protection Program activity within the Clean Air and Climate program area. The $7.8 million requested for the Climate Protection Program for FY2013 is $8.6 million (53.0%) less than the FY2012 appropriation of $16.3 million. The net reduction is the result of the proposed elimination of the Clean Automotive Technology (CAT) program in FY2013.[92] The $7.8 million requested for the Climate Change Program activity for FY2013, reflects a reallocation of a portion of the resources (including technical experts) that previously supported the CAT program FY2012, to support the growing implementation and compliance activities associated with National Highway Traffic Safety Administration (NHTSA) Corporate Average Fuel Economy (CAFE) and EPA greenhouse gas (GHG) emission standards for light-duty and heavy-duty vehicles and engines, and to support GHG standard setting actions regarding advanced vehicle and engine technologies, including light-duty and heavy-duty trucks.

The largest dollar increase for FY2013 above the FY2012 level within the S&T account was the $101.9 million for Federal Vehicle and Fuel Standards and Certification within the Clean Air and Climate program area, $10.0 million (11%) above the FY2012 enacted amount. Additionally within the S&T account, the FY2013 request included $121.2 million for Safe and Sustainable Water (SSW) Research, a $7.7 million (6.8%) increase above FY2012, and $105.9 million for Air, Climate, and Energy (ACE) Research, a $7.0 million (7.1%) increase. Primarily contributing to these two requested increases are $4.3 million and $3.8 million increases requested above FY2012 under SSW and ACE research program activities respectively, as part of EPA's overall $14.1 million request within the S&T account to address additional questions regarding the safety of hydraulic fracturing (HF).[93] HF has been an area of considerable interest during the 112th Congress.[94] The research, a collaborative effort between DOE and USGS under a Memorandum of Understanding that is under development, includes an assessment of potential air, ecosystem, and water quality impacts of hydraulic fracturing.

---

[91] Under the Bioterrorism Act of 2002, and Homeland Security Presidential Directives 7, 9, and 10, EPA is the lead federal agency for coordinating security of the nation's water systems, and plays a role in developing early warning monitoring and decontamination capabilities associated with potential attacks using biological contaminants.

[92] See footnote 89, EPA's FY2013 Congressional Justification, PDF pp. 88-90.

[93] See footnote 89, EPA's FY2013 Congressional Justification, PDF pp. 36, 157-159, and 166-169.

[94] For example, see House Committee on Science, Space and Technology-Energy and Environment Subcommittee February 1, 2012, hearing "EPA Hydraulic Fracturing Research," http://science house.gov/hearing/energy-and-environment-subcommittee-epa-hydraulic-fracturing-research. See also testimony and discussion Congressional hearings regarding FY2013 Budget Request for EPA: February 29, 2012, House Committee on Appropriations, Interior, Environment, and Related Agencies Subcommittee, http://appropriations house.gov/Calendar/EventSingle.aspx?EventID=277064; and February 28, 2012, House Energy and Commerce Committee, Subcommittee on Energy and Power and the Subcommittee on Environment and the Economy, http://energycommerce.house.gov/hearings/hearingdetail.aspx?NewsID=9317.

The activities funded within the S&T account include research conducted by universities, foundations, and other non-federal entities that receive EPA grants, and research conducted by the agency at its own laboratories and facilities. R&D at EPA headquarters and laboratories around the country, as well as external R&D, is managed primarily by EPA's Office of Research and Development (ORD). A large portion of the S&T account funds EPA's R&D activities managed by ORD, including the agency's research laboratories and research grants. The account also provides funding for the agency's applied science and technology activities conducted through its program offices (e.g., the Office of Water). Many of the programs implemented by other offices within EPA have a research component, but the research is not necessarily the primary focus of the program.

The EPA S&T account incorporates elements of the former EPA Research and Development account, as well as a portion of the former Salaries and Expenses, and Program Operations accounts, which had been in place until FY1996.[95] Although the Office of Management and Budget (OMB) reports[96] historical and projected budget authority (BA) amounts for R&D at EPA (and other federal agencies), OMB documents do not describe how these amounts explicitly relate to the requested and appropriated funding amounts for the many specific EPA program activities. The R&D BA amounts reported by OMB are typically significantly less than amounts appropriated/requested for the S&T account as a whole. (BA as reported by OMB is included in **Table 16** below for purposes of comparison.) This is an indication that not all of the EPA S&T account funding is allocated to R&D.

In addition to funding priorities among the various EPA programs and activities, several recent and pending EPA regulatory actions[97] were central to the debate on the FY2012 appropriations, including EPA scientific research in support of these actions. These issues continue to be prominent in the debate regarding the FY2013 appropriations as interest in the potential impacts of EPA regulations has continued.[98] Actions under the Clean Air Act, in particular EPA controls on emissions of greenhouse gases, as well as efforts to address conventional pollutants from a number of industries, received much of the attention during the FY2012 appropriations debate. Several actions under the Clean Water Act, Safe Drinking Water Act, and Resource Conservation and Recovery Act (RCRA) also received some attention. Congressional concerns regarding these issues were prominent areas of debate during EPA S&T oversight and FY2012 appropriations deliberations. Some Members expressed concerns related to these actions during hearings and markup of EPA's FY2012 appropriations,[99] and authorizing committees continue to address EPA regulatory actions through hearings and legislation.

---

[95] In recent years, EPA's annual appropriations have been requested, considered, and enacted according to eight statutory appropriations accounts established by Congress during the FY1996 appropriations process. Because of the differences in the scope of the activities included in these accounts, apt comparisons before and after FY1996 are difficult.

[96] The Office of Management and Budget (OMB) reports R&D budget authority (BA) amounts in its Analytical Perspectives accompanying the annual President's budget request. See OMB, *Fiscal Year 2013 Budget of the United States: Analytical Perspectives—Special Topics/Research and Development,* pp. 365-371, http://www.whitehouse.gov/sites/default/files/omb/budget/fy2013/assets/topics.pdf.

[97] See CRS Report R41561, *EPA Regulations: Too Much, Too Little, or On Track?*, by James E. McCarthy and Claudia Copeland, for a discussion of selected EPA regulatory actions.

[98] See hearings on EPA FY2013 budget request cited in footnote 94.

[99] See CRS Report R41979, *Environmental Protection Agency (EPA) FY2012 Appropriations: Overview of Provisions in H.R. 2584 as Reported,* by Robert Esworthy.

The Consolidated Appropriations Act, 2012 (P.L. 112-74, H.R. 2055) included several administrative and general provisions affecting EPA actions and authorities.[100] Along with the provisions contained in P.L. 112-74, the Conference Report (H.Rept. 112-331 on H.R. 2055) included extensive language with regard to specific actions by EPA, in lieu of certain provisions proposed in the House Appropriations Committee-reported bill (H.R. 2584) for FY2012. With regard to EPA's R&D, under the S&T account in H.Rept. 112-331 (p. 1072), the Conferees required specific refinements and modifications to EPA's policies and practices for conducting assessments under the agency's Integrated Risk Information System (IRIS).

Some Members of Congress and other stakeholders have consistently raised concerns about the adequacy of funding for scientific research at EPA. The adequacy of funding for this purpose has been part of a broader question about the adequacy of overall federal funding for a broad range of scientific research activities administered by multiple federal agencies. Some Members, state agencies, scientists, and environmental and other stakeholder organizations have expressed concerns about the downward trend in federal resources for scientific research over time. Central facets of this debate include the question of whether the regulatory actions of federal agencies are based on "sound science" and how scientific research is applied in developing federal policy. Some Members have also raised concerns that EPA's scientific justifications for several of its rules and regulations have been scrutinized recently as a result of apprehensions regarding quality of data, lack of transparency and effective peer review, and other related research planning and process issues.[101]

Table 16. Environmental Protection Agency S&T Account

(in millions of dollars)

Environmental Protection Agency	FY2011 Enacted (P.L. 112-10)[a]	FY2012 Enacted (P.L. 112-74)[a]	FY2013 Request
Science and Technology Approps. Account			
Air Toxics and Quality	$120.5	—	—
Clean Air and Climate	—	124.4	127.1
- Climate Protection Program	—	16.3	7.8
Climate Protection	16.8	—	—
Enforcement	15.3	15.3	15.6

[100] For example, Division E, Title IV "General Provisions" in P.L. 112-74, included provisions specifying requirements and restrictions on the use of FY2012 funds for certain Clean Air Act regulatory actions and greenhouse gas emission reporting requirements (see sections 425, 426, 427 and 432), and certain Clean Water Act permitting requirements associated with silvicultural activities (section 429). CRS Report R42332, *Environmental Protection Agency (EPA) FY2012 Appropriations*, by Robert Esworthy, contains tables comparing EPA provisions contained in P.L. 112-74 with those proposed in the Interior, Environment, and Related Agencies Appropriations bill H.R. 2584 (H.Rept. 112-151) as reported by the House Committee on Appropriations on July 19, 2011. The House considered H.R. 2584 from July 25, 2011, to July 28, 2011, but did not complete debate on the bill.

[101] For example, see hearings held by the House Committee on Science, Space, and Technology, Subcommittee on Energy and Environment: February 3, 2012, entitled "Fostering Quality Science at EPA: Perspectives on Common Sense Reform – Day II," http://science.house.gov/hearing/energy-and-environment-subcommittee-hearing-fostering-quality-science-epa-perspectives-0; and November 17, 2011, entitled "Fostering Quality Science at EPA: The Need for Common Sense Reform," http://science.house.gov/hearing/energy-and-environment-subcommittee-hearing-fostering-quality-science-epa-perspectives.

Environmental Protection Agency	FY2011 Enacted (P.L. 112-10)ᵃ	FY2012 Enacted (P.L. 112-74)ᵃ	FY2013 Request
Homeland Security	46.2	42.0	40.1
Indoor Air and Radiation	1.3	6.8	6.7
IT/Data Management/Security	3.7	3.7	4.0
Operations & Administration	69.7	72.0	75.5
Pesticide Licensing	6.6	6.6	7.1
Research: Air, Climate, and Energy	—	98.8	105.9
Research: Clean Air	102.4	—	—
- *Research: Global Change*	*20.8*	—	—
Research: Safe and Sustainable Water	117.3	113.5	121.2
Research: Human Health & Ecosystems	243.9	—	—
Research: Chemical Safety and Sustainability	—	131.3	134.7
- *Research: Computational toxicology*	*21.1*	*21.2*	*21.3*
- *Research: Endocrine disruptor*	*16.0*	*16.9*	*16.3*
- *Research: Fellowships*	*16.0*	*Not specified*	*Not specified*
Research: Land Protection	13.4	—	—
Research: Sustainability	25.5	—	—
Research: Pesticides and Toxics	27.3	—	—
Research: Sustainable and Healthy Communities	—	170.7	165.7
Water: Human Health Protection	3.8	3.8	3.6
Research: National Priorities (Water Quality and Availability)	—	5.0	0.0
—Subtotal S&T Account Base Appropriations	***$813.5***	***$793.7***	***$807.3***
—Transfer in from Hazardous Substance Superfund Account	***$26.8***	***$23.0***	***$23.2***
Total Science and Technology	**$840.3**	**$816.7**	**$830.5**
R&D Budget Authority Reported by OMB	*(CR) $584.0*	*$568.0 est.*	*$580.0 est.*

Source: Prepared by CRS. FY2011 enacted amounts in the table are based on the prior year amounts presented in the Conference Report (H.Rept. 112-331 on H.R. 2055) for the Consolidated Appropriations Act, FY2012 (P.L. 112-74) and include a 0.2% across-the-board rescission. FY2012 enacted and FY2013 requested amounts are based on the EPA "FY2013 Justification of Appropriation Estimate for Committee on Appropriations," http://www.epa.gov/planandbudget/annualplan/fy2013.html#FY13budget. The FY2012 enacted amounts as reported in the EPA justification reflect the subsequent application of the 0.16% across-the-board rescission required by Section 436 of P.L. 112-74. OMB amounts of R&D budget authority are as reported in OMB *Fiscal Year 2013 Budget of the United States: Analytical Perspectives—Special Topics/Research and Development*, pp. 365-371, http://www.whitehouse.gov/sites/default/files/omb/budget/fy2013/assets/topics.pdf. Totals may differ from the sum of the components due to rounding. N/A = not available.

Note:

a.   Includes rescissions.

Department of Transportation[102]

President Obama has requested $1.076 billion for Department of Transportation (DOT) R&D in FY2013, an increase of $132 million (14.0%) from the FY2012 enacted level. (See **Table 17**.) Two DOT agencies—the Federal Highway Administration (FHWA) and the Federal Aviation Administration (FAA)—account for most of the department's R&D funding (82% in the FY2013 request).

The FAA budget justification[103] reflects a request for $354.0 million for R&D and R&D facilities in FY2013, a decrease of $12.7 million (3.5%) from the FY2012 enacted level.[104] The request includes $180.0 million for Research, Engineering, and Development (RE&D), an increase of $12.4 million (7.4%) above the FY2012 level. The Senate Committee on Appropriations recommends $160.0 million for RE&D, a decrease of $7.6 million (-4.5%) below the FY2012 enacted level, and $20 million (-11.1%) below the request. The NextGen R&D portfolio is funded at $67 million in the President's FY2013 budget (up $7.3 million (12.2%) from the FY2012 level).[105] The Senate Committee on Appropriations recommends $54.9 million for NextGen R&D, $4.9 (-8.2%) million less than the FY2012 enacted level, and $12.1 million (-18.1%) less than the request. Under the President's budget, the FAA's Environment and Energy program (including funding for NextGen environmental research, aircraft technologies fuel, and metrics) would receive $34.6 million in FY2013, down $3.9 million (-10.2%) from FY2012. The Senate Committee on Appropriations recommends $35.1 million, down $3.5 million (-9.1%) from FY2012 and up $0.4 million (1.2%) from the FY2013 request.

The FHWA would receive $528.4 million in R&D funding in FY2013 under the President's request, an increase of $116.9 million (28.4%). Highway Research and Development funding would increase to $200.0 million, up $45.0 million (29.0%) from FY2012 funding of $155.0 million. Funding for Intelligent Transportation Systems R&D would increase to $94.6 million in FY2013, up $8.2 million (9.5%) from its FY2012 funding level. Two new efforts, the Multimodal Innovation Research Program and the University Transportation Center Multimodal Competitive Research Grants program, would each receive $20 million in FY2013. In addition, R&D funding for the State Planning and Research program would grow to $177.5 million in FY2013, up $23.7 million (15.4%) over FY2012. The Senate Committee on Appropriations recommends $429.8 million for "transportation research," which it states is the same as the FY2012 enacted level.[106] This appropriation appears to incorporate a different set of activities than what the Administration characterizes as R&D. According to S.Rept. 112-157, this funding would support the transportation research and technology programs of the FHWA, as well as intelligent

---

[102] This section was written by John F. Sargent, Specialist in Science and Technology Policy, CRS Resources, Science, and Industry Division.

[103] FAA, *Budget Estimates Fiscal Year 2013: Federal Aviation Administration*, http://www.dot.gov/budget/2013/faa_%20fy_%202013_budget_estimate.pdf.

[104] Data provided by OMB to CRS on February 14, 2012 shows FAA R&D funding requested for FY2013 to be $326 million.

[105] According to the FAA, this funding supports NextGen-specific research into wake turbulence, human factors, and 'clean' aircraft technologies, as well as $12 million for the Joint Planning and Development Office for the coordination of interagency initiatives. See Federal Highway Administration, U.S. Department of Transportation, *Budget Estimates Fiscal Year2013*, February 2012.

[106] S.Rept. 112-57.

transportation systems; surface transportation research; technology deployment, training, and education; university transportation research; and the Bureau of Transportation Statistics.

The DOT budget seeks to replace the Research and Innovative Technology Administration (RITA) with an Office of the Assistant Secretary for Research and Technology in the office of the Secretary. The department asserts that this will "strengthen research functions across the Department by providing a prominent centralized focus on research and technology, which will improve collaboration and coordination among operating administrations."[107]

Table 17. Department of Transportation R&D

(in millions of dollars)

	FY2011 Actual	FY2012 Enacted	FY2013 Request	S. 2322 Committee-reported[a]
Federal Highway Administration[b]	448	411	528	n/a
Federal Aviation Administration	334	367	326	n/a
Other DOT agencies	171	166	222	n/a
Total, DOT R&D[c]	953	944	1,076	n/a

Source: DOT FY2011 agency budget justifications; unpublished tables provided by OMB to CRS in February 2010; email communication between OMB and CRS. FY2013 Senate Committee-reported from S. 2322 as reported and S.Rept. 112-157.

Notes:

a. R&D levels cannot be determined from bill or report language.

b. Analysis of special data run provided by OMB to CRS on February 14, 2012.

c. Totals may differ from the sum of the components due to rounding.

---

[107] U.S. Department of Transportation, *Budget Highlights: Fiscal Year 2013*, http://www.dot.gov/budget/2013/dot_budget_highlights_fy_2013.pdf.

Author Contact Information

John F. Sargent Jr., Coordinator
Specialist in Science and Technology Policy
jsargent@crs.loc.gov, 7-9147

Robert Esworthy
Specialist in Environmental Policy
resworthy@crs.loc.gov, 7-7236

Heather B. Gonzalez
Specialist in Science and Technology Policy
hgonzalez@crs.loc.gov, 7-1895

Christine M. Matthews
Specialist in Science and Technology Policy
cmatthews@crs.loc.gov, 7-7055

Daniel Morgan
Specialist in Science and Technology Policy
dmorgan@crs.loc.gov, 7-5849

John D. Moteff
Specialist in Science and Technology Policy
jmoteff@crs.loc.gov, 7-1435

Wendy H. Schacht
Specialist in Science and Technology Policy
wschacht@crs.loc.gov, 7-7066

Pamela W. Smith
Analyst in Biomedical Policy
psmith@crs.loc.gov, 7-7048

Harold F. Upton
Analyst in Natural Resources Policy
hupton@crs.loc.gov, 7-2264